CHILD DEVELOPMENT

CHILD DEVELOPMENT

(In 3 Volumes)

Experimental Child Psychology

(Volume-1)

Dr. Sujata Mittal

ISHA BOOKS
DELHI-110 033

Child Development

ISBN: 81-8205-085-5 (Set)
ISBN: 81-8205-086-3 (Vol. 1)

Published in 2004 in India by
Isha Books, D-43, Prithviraj Road,
Adarsh Nagar, Delhi-110 033

Laser Typesetting at : *Shree Vaishnavi Creations*, Delhi
Printed at : Chawla Offset Press, Delhi

Contents

Preface

Children are our legacy for the future. The better we understand their thinking, feeling, and behaviour, the more likely we will be to maximize their development. Almost all children grow up in a family. They interact with a mother or a father or both. Many have brothers or sisters. The personalities and lives of the people close to a child affect the child and in turn the child affects those around him or her. This mutual influence process makes understanding children both challenging and exciting.

In today's fast-life, children are subjected for emotional disorders, which are caused by several reasons. Conflicts of ideas or opinions, quarrel in the family, constant failures in achieving the goal, constantly getting abused and ill treated by the master or mistress, severe anxiety or worry, deep sense of sadness due to loss of livelihood, strong feeling of destitute, a feeling that he/she became an orphan, socially disowned, all these are common causes of behaviour disorders. Child psychology studies systematically about these disorders and offer appropriate solutions.

Some of the major mental and emotional disorders of children and the appropriate treatment technologies for them are elaboratively described in this book. Written in a lucid style, this book relates psychological knowledge to practical situations, showing what psychology has to offer in real life situations involving children. This book will be highly useful to scholars, academics, educationists and psychologists.

Editor

1

Cognitive Theories of Child Behaviour

The recent years have witnessed a resurgence of interest in self-referent phenomena. Selfprocesses have come to pervade diverse domains of psychology because most external influences affect human functioning through intermediary self processes rather than directly. The self system thus lies at the very heart of causal processes. Personal factors are very much involved in regulating attentional processes, schematic processing of experiences, memory representation and reconstruction, cognitively-based motivation, emotion activation, psychobiologic functioning and the efficacy with which cognitive and behavioral competencies are executed in the transactions of everyday life. In the agentic sociocognitive view, people are self-organizing, proactive, self-reflecting, and self-regulating, not just reactive organisms shaped and shepherded by external events. People have the power to influence their own actions to produce certain results. The capacity to exercise control over one's thought processes, motivation, affect, and action operates through mechanisms of personal agency.

Human agency has been conceptualised in at least three different ways—as either autonomous agency, mechanically reactive agency or emergent interactive agency. The notion that humans operate as entirely independent agents has few serious advocates, although it is sometimes invoked in caricatures of cognitive theories of human behavior. The tools for the exercise of agency are derived, in large part, from experiences but what is created by their generative use is not reducible to those experiences. Human action, being socially situated, is the product of a dynamic interplay of personal and situational influences.

Another approach to the self system is to construe it as mechanically reactive agency. It is an internal system through which external influences operate mechanistically on action, but individuals exert no motivative, self-reflective, self-reactive, creative or directive influence on the process. The self system is merely a repository for implanted structures and a conduit for external influences. The more dynamic models operating holistically include multilevel neural networks. However, a diverse mix of parallel distributed neural activity cannot remain fragmented. It requires an integrative system. Given the proactive nature of human functioning, such a system must have agentic capabilities as well as integrative reactive ones. Agentic functions get lodged in a hidden network operating without any consciousness. Consciousness is the very substance of phenomenal and functional mental life. It provides the information base for thinking about events, planning, constructing courses of action and reflecting on the adequacy of one's thinking and actions.

There is an important difference between being conscious of the experiences one is undergoing, and consciously producing given experiences. Consciousness of one's heart rate and consciously and intentionally doing things known to elevate one's heart rate illustrate the difference between passive undergoing and agentic doing. The purposive accessing and deliberative processing of information to fashion efficacious courses of action represent the functional consciousness. Consciousness cannot be reduced to an epiphenomenon of the output of a mental process realised mechanically at nonconscious lower levels.

In the connectionist line of theorizing, sensory organs deliver up information through their diverse pathways to the hidden network acting as the cognitive agent that does the construing, planning, motivating and regulating. However, stripped of consciousness and agentic capability of decision and action, people are mere automatons undergoing actions devoid of any subjectivity, conscious regulation, phenomenological life, or personal identity. In their view, people do not act on beliefs, goals, aspirations and expectations. Rather, activation of their network structure makes them do things.

Cognitive factors do quite well in accounting for variance in human behavior and guiding successful interventions. To make their way successfully through a complex world, people have to make sound judgments about their capabilities, anticipate the probable effects of different events and actions, ascertain sociostructural opportunities and constraints and regulate their behavior accordingly. These belief systems represent a working model of the world that enables people to achieve desired results and avoid untoward ones. Reflective and forethoughtful capabilities are, therefore, vital for survival and progress. Agentic factors that are explanatory, predictive, and of demonstrated functional value may be translatable, refinable and modeled in another theoretical language but not eliminatable.

In social cognitive theory, people are agentic operators in their life course not just onlooking hosts of internal mechanisms orchestrated by environmental events. They are sentient agents of experiences rather than simply undergoers of experiences. The sensory, motor and cerebral systems are tools people use to accomplish the tasks and goals that give meaning and direction to their lives. Agentic action shapes brain development and functioning throughout the life course. It is not just exposure to stimulation, but agentic action in exploring, manipulating and influencing the environment that counts. By regulating their own motivation and the activities they pursue, people produce the experiences that form the neurobiological substrate of symbolic, social, psychomotor and other skills.

Social cognitive theory subscribes to a model of emergent interactive agency. Persons are neither autonomous agents nor simply mechanical conveyers of animating environmental influences. Mental events are brain activities not immaterial entities existing apart from neural systems. However, materialism does not imply reductionism of psychology to biology. Knowing how the biological machinery works, tells one little on how to orchestrate that machinery psychosocially for diverse purposes.

Knowledge of the brain circuitry involved in learning says little about how best to devise conditions of learning in terms of levels of abstractness, novelty, and challenge; how to provide incentives to get people to attend to, process, and organize relevant information; in what modes to present information; and whether learning is better achieved independently, cooperatively, or competitively. The optimal conditions must be specified by psychological principles and are not derivable from neurophysiological theory because it does not contain the relevant psychosocial factors in its subject matter. To use an analogy, the agentic software is not reducable to the biological hardware. Each is governed by its own set of principles requiring explication in its own right. In a nondualistic mentalism, thought processes are emergent brain activities that are not ontologically reducible. Emergent properties differ qualitatively from their constituent elements. Through their interactive effects they are transformed into new phenomena. One must distinguish between the physical basis of thought and its functional properties. Cognitive processes are not only emergent brain activities; they also exert determinative influence.

The human mind is generative, creative, proactive, and self-reflective not just reactive. The dignified burial of the dualistic Descartes, brings to the fore the more formidable explanatory challenge for a physicalistic theory of human agency. It must explain how people operate as thinkers of the thoughts that serve determinative functions. They construct thoughts about future courses of action to suit ever changing situations, assess their likely functional value, organise and deploy strategically the selected options and evaluate the adequacy of their thinking based on the effects their actions produce. In the exercise of personal agency people actuate the brain processes for realizing selected intentions. Theorists seeking explanations of human behavior at the neurophysiological level must address such agentic activities as forethought, intention, aspiration, proaction, creativity, self-appraisal and self-reflection and their functional neural circuitry.

Human behavior has often been explained in terms of one-sided determinism. In such modes of unidirectional causation, behavior is depicted as being shaped and controlled by environmental influences or driven by internal dispositions.

Social cognitive theory explains psychosocial functioning in terms of triadic reciprocal causation. The term causation is used to mean functional dependence between events. In this model of reciprocal causality, internal personal factors in the form of cognitive, affective and biological events; behavioral patterns; and environmental events all operate as interacting determinants that influence one another bidirectionally. In triadic causation there is no fixed pattern for reciprocal interaction. Rather, the relative contribution of each of the constituent classes of influences depends on the activities, situational circumstances, and sociostructural constraints and opportunities.

The environment is not a monolithic entity. Social cognitive theory distinguishes between three types of environmental structures. They include the imposed environment, selected environment, and constructed environment. Gradations of environmental changeability require the exercise of increasing levels of personal agency. The imposed physical and sociostructural environment is thrust upon people whether they like it or not. Although they have little control over its presence, they have leeway in how they construe it and react to it. There is a major difference between the potential environment and the environment people actually experience. For the most part, the environment is only a potentiality whose rewarding and punishing aspects do not come into being until the environment is selectively activated by appropriate courses of action. Which part of the potential environment becomes the actual experienced environment thus depends on how people behave.

The choice of associates, activities and milieus constitutes the selected environment. The environments that are created do not exist as a potentiality waiting to be selected and activated. Rather, people construct social environments and institutional systems through their generative efforts. The construal, selection and construction of environments affect the nature of the reciprocal interplay among personal, behavioral and environmental factors. Unidirectional causality emphasizing either dispositionalism or situationalism eventually gave way to reciprocal models of causation. Nowadays almost everyone is an interactionist. The major issues in contention center on the type of interactionism espoused. At least three different interactional models have been posed, two of which subscribe to one-way causation in the link to behavior. The major weakness with this causal model is that personal and environmental influences do not function as independent determinants. They affect each other. People create, alter and destroy environments. The changes they produce in environmental conditions, in turn, affect them personally. The unidirectional causality with regard to behavior is another serious deficiency of this model of interactionism.

The partially bidirectional conception of interaction, which is now widely adopted in personality theory, acknowledges that persons and situations affect each other. But, this model treats influences relating to behavior as flowing in only one direction. The person-situation interchange undirectionally produces behavior, but the behavior itself does not affect the ongoing transaction between the person and the situation. A major limitation of this interactional causal model is that behavior is not procreated by an intimate interchange between a behaviorless person and the environment. Such a feat would be analogous to immaculate conception. Except through their social stimulus value, people cannot affect their environment other than through their actions. Their behavior plays a dominant role in how they influence situations which, in turn, affect their thoughts, emotional reactions and behavior. In short, behavior is an interacting determinant rather than a detached by-product of a behaviorless person-situation interchange.

Social cognitive theory conceptualizes the interactional causal structure as triadic reciprocal causation. It involves a dynamic interplay among personal determinants, behavior and environmental influences. Efforts to verify every possible interactant simultaneously would produce experimental paralysis. However, because of the time lags in the operation of the triadic factors one can gain understanding of how different segments of reciprocal causation function. Different subspecialties of psychology center their inquiry on selected segments of triadic reciprocality. Cognitive psychologists examine the interactive relation between thought and action as their major sector of interest. Social psychologists examine mainly the segment of reciprocality between the person and the environment in the triadic system. This line of inquiry adds to understanding of how environmental influences in the form of social persuasion, modeling, and tuition alter cognitions and affective proclivities.

The reciprocal element in the person-environment segment of causation is of central interest to the subspecialty of person perception. People evoke different reactions from their social environment by their physical characteristics, such as their age, size, race, sex and physical attractiveness even before they say or do anything. They similarly activate different reactions depending on their socially conferred roles and status.

The social reactions so elicited, in turn, affect the recipients' conceptions of themselves and others in ways that either strengthen or weaken the environmental bias. Of all the different segments in the triadic causal structure, historically the reciprocal interplay between behavior and environmental events has received the greatest attention. Indeed, ethological, transactional and behavioristic theories focus almost exclusively on this portion of reciprocity in the explanation of behavior.

In the transactions of everyday life, behavior alters environmental conditions, and behavior is, in turn, altered by the very conditions it creates. The bidirectional relation between behavior and environment is not disembodied from thought, however. Consider coercive parent-child interactions. In discordant families, coercive actions by one member tend to elicit coercive counteractions from the partner in mutually escalating aggression. But about half the time coercion does not produce coercive counteractions. To understand fully the interactive relation between behavior and social environment, the analysis must be extended temporally and broadened to include cognitive determinants operating in the triadic interlocking system.

This requires tapping into what people are thinking as they perform actions and experience their effects.

Counterresponses to antecedent acts are influenced not only by their immediate effects but also by people's judgments of eventual outcomes should they stick to that course of action. Thus, aggressive children will continue or even escalate their coercive behavior, although immediately punished, when they expect persistence eventually to gain them what they seek. But the same momentary punishment will serve as an inhibitor, rather than as an escalator, of coercion when they expect that the continuance of the aversive conduct will be ineffective. Thus, in acting on their environment, people think about where their actions are likely to lead and what they eventually produce. Forethought partly governs the form the reciprocal interplay between behavior and environment takes. Combining knowledge of the various subsystems of causality increases understanding of the superordinate causal system.

Some progress has been made in clarifying how the triadic determinants operate together and how their patterning and relative strength change in the causal structure over time. These studies involve microanalyses of triadic reciprocal causation in which people manage a dynamic computerized environment. Each of the major interactants in the triadic causal structure-personal, behavioral, and environmental-functions as an important constituent in the transactional system.

The personal determinant is indexed by self-beliefs of efficacy, cognized goals, quality of analytic thinking, and affective self-reactions. The options that are actually executed in the management of the organizational environment constitute the behavioral determinant. The properties of the organizational environment, the level of challenge it prescribes, and its responsiveness to behavioral interventions represent the environmental determinant.

The constituent factors in the ongoing transactional system are measured repeatedly to verify the dynamics of the triadic causal system over time. The findings clarify the way in which the interlocked set of determinants operate as a whole and change in their relative contribution with experience.

Role of Fortuitous Determinants

The role of fortuitous determinants in causal structures remains ever dormant in psychological theorizing even though it is often a critical factor in the paths lives take. People are often brought together through a fortuitous constellation of events that set in motion reciprocal interplays of influences that shape the course of their lives. Indeed, some of the most important determinants of life paths often arise through the most trivial of circumstances. In these instances, seemingly minor events have important and enduring impact on the courses that lives take. Consider an example that illustrates prospectively the branching power of fortuitous events in the formation of a marital partnership.

A fortuitous event in socially mediated happenstances is defined as an unintended meeting of persons unfamiliar with each other. Although the separate chains of events in a chance encounter have their own causal determinants, their intersection occurs fortuitously rather than by design. It is not that a fortuitous event is uncaused but, rather, there is a lot of randomness to the determining conditions of its intersections. The profusion of separate chains of events in everyday life provides numerous opportunities for such fortuitous intersects.

People are often inaugurated into marital partnerships, occupational careers, or untoward life paths through circumstances.

A happenstance meeting launches a new life trajectory. Had the chance encounter not occurred, the participants lives would have taken quite different courses. The power of most fortuitous influences lies not in the properties of the events themselves but in the interactive processes they initiate. These branching processes are in accord with chaos theory in which minor events set in motion cyclic processes that eventuate in major changes. Of the myriad fortuitous elements encountered in daily life, many of them touch people only lightly, others leave more lasting effects, and still others thrust people into new life trajectories.

Psychological science cannot foretell the occurrence of fortuitous intersects, except in a very general way. Personal proclivities, the social circles in which one moves, and the kinds of people who populate those settings make some types of intersects more probable than others.

However, social cognitive theory provides a conceptual scheme for predicting the nature, scope, and strength of the impact that chance encounters will have on human lives based on the reciprocal interplay of personal attributes and the characteristics of the social milieus into which one is inaugurated. The personal determinants of the impact of fortuitous encounters operate by converting chance meetings into ongoing relationships. People's attributes, interests, and skills will affect whether they can gain sufficient social acceptance and satisfaction to sustain involvement with those they happened to encounter. Emotional ties also play an influential role. Interpersonal attraction seals chance encounters into lasting bonds.

Values and personal standards similarly come into play. Fortuitous meetings are more apt to last if the persons involved have similar value commitments and evaluative standards than if they clash. The social determinants of the impact of fortuitous encounters concern the holding and shaping power of the milieus into which people are fortuitously inaugurated. Individuals become attached to groups that provide valued benefits and rewards but forsake those that have little to offer. Fortuitous induction into a group also provides a new symbolic environment designed to foster affinity, solidarity, and shape ideological perspectives on life.

The belief system of milieus and their reach and degree of closedness operate as other formative environmental factors. Chance encounters have the greatest potential for abruptly branching people into new trajectories of life when they induct them into a relatively closed milieu. A totalistic environment supplies a pervading new reality-new kinships, strongly held group beliefs and values, all-encompassing codes of conduct, and substantial rewarding and coercive power to alter the entire course of personal lives.

People can make chance happen by pursuing an active life that increases the number of fortuitous encounters they are likely to experience. Indeed, Austin highlights the role of action in chance occurrences. In the proactive sociocognitive view, chance favors the inquisitive, venturesome and persistent. By selecting advantageous activities and milieus people can make chance occurrences work for them. Social scientists underplay fortuitous determinants in their theoretical schemes, but such factors figure significantly in their prescriptions for personal development.

On the utilization side, the proactive efforts center on cultivating personal attributes that enable people to make the most of opportunities that arise unexpectedly from time to time. Pasteur put it well when he noted that "Chance favors only the prepared mind." On the nullifying side, people are equipped with self-protective capabilities that enable them to resist social traps leading down detrimental paths, and to extricate themselves from such predicaments should they become enmeshed in them. At the societal level, they create social systems that provide opportunity structures for beneficial fortuities and institute safeguards that set limits on coercive control in detrimental fortuities. Mastering the tools of personal agency does not necessarily assure a desired future. But these types of personal and institutional measures give people a greater hand in shaping their own destinies.

Personal Determinants

The field of personality has traditionally relied heavily on all-purpose measures of personal attributes in efforts to explain how personal factors contribute to psychosocial functioning. In this "one fits all approach," the items are decontextualized by deleting information about the situations with which people are dealing. The predictiveness of indefinite global measures will depend on the extent to which the visualized activities and contextual factors on which the mental averaging is performed happen to overlap with those being studied.

The everyday realities that people must manage are structured and operate conditionally. Thus, behaving assertively with indifferent store clerks will bring more attentive service, whereas confrontive assertiveness toward police officers will get one roughed up or arrested. As a consequence, people will behave assertively with clerks but compliantly with police. A shapeless overall rating is ill-equipped to explain and predict the variation in assertiveness under these different circumstances. Given the highly conditional nature of human functioning, it is unrealistic to expect personality measures cast in nonconditional generalities to shed much light on the contribution of personal factors to psychosocial functioning in different task domains under diverse circumstances across all situations. Indeed, personality measures that capture the contextualized and multifaceted nature of personal causation within an agentic model have greater explanatory and predictive power and provide more effective guides for personal change than do global trait measures.

The convenience of all purpose global tests of personal determinants is gained at the cost of explanatory and predictive power. A major movement in psychology is away from global structures to more domain-linked knowledge structures, self-conceptions, and competencies. Even in the field of cognitive development, the bulwark of global structuralism is being abandoned for more specialized cognitive competencies. It is ironic that, at a time when other subfields of psychology are becoming contextualized and discarding global personal structures for more particularized ones, much of the field of personality is seeking the personal causes of human behavior in omnibus conglomerate traits severed from the social realities of everyday life. The multifaceted dynamic nature of personal causation raises the broader issue of how personal determinants are conceptualized and measured.

The influence of personal factors on human functioning is often insufficiently recognized because the issue tends to be construed in static terms of individual differences rather than personal determination of action. The issue of major interest for the science of personality is not how differences between individuals on a behavioral continuum correlate with behavior, but rather how personal factors operate in causal structures in producing and regulating behavior under the highly contingent conditions of everyday life. Consider a situation in which a personal factor is essential for certain types of performances but is developed to the same high level in different individuals.

The difference among individuals is negligible and would, therefore, not correlate with performance because of constricted variability. However, the personal competence is, in fact, vital for successful performance. For example, all librarians know how to read well and do not differ in this respect, but possessing the ability to read is indispensable for performing the librarianship role. Low correlations between "individual differences" in a personal determinant and performance resulting from curtailed variability are often misinterpreted as evidence that personal factors exert little causal impact. Personal determinants operate as multifaceted dynamic factors in causal structures rather than as static entities that people possess in differing amounts. These alternative perspectives on personal causation reflect more than differences in semantic labeling.

The individual differences approach is rooted in trait theory, whereas the personal determinants approach is founded on an agentic model of functional relations between dynamic personal factors that govern the quality of human adaptation and change.

Social cognitive theory does not cede the construct of "disposition" to trait theory. Dynamic dispositions must be distinguished from static trait dispositions. Individuals who have a resilient sense of efficacy in a given domain are disposed to behave differently in that realm of activity from those who are beset by self-doubt. Efficacy beliefs are patterned differently across individuals and spheres of activity.

The issue in contention is not whether people have personal dispositions but how they are conceptualized and operationalized.

In social cognitive theory, an efficacious personality disposition is a dynamic, multifaceted belief system that varies across different activity domains and under different situational demands rather than being a decontextualized conglomerate. The patterned individuality of efficacy beliefs represents the unique dispositional makeup of efficaciousness for any given person. In social cognitive theory, dispositions are personal factors such as self-beliefs, aspirations, and outcome expectations that regulate behavior rather then descriptors of habitual behavior.

Conceptions of Personality

Theorizing in personality often contains a variety of dualities that social cognitive theory rejects. It will be recalled from the earlier discussion that the theory casts off mind-body dualism. Mental events are brain activities rather than immaterial entities that exist apart from brain processes. There are other forms, the dualistic conceptions of which are discussed briefly in the sections that follow.

One common dichotomy separates self into agent and object. People are said to be agents when they act on the environment but objects when they reflect and act on themselves. Social cognitive theory questions such a dualistic view of self. Proaction does not operate isolatedly from self-reaction. The dual functions of the self typically operate interactively. In their daily transactions, people formulate courses of action, anticipate their likely effects, and act on their judgments. While acting on their environment, they are also evaluating and reacting to themselves. They monitor and analyze how well their thinking and corresponding actions have served them and change their strategies accordingly.

One is just as much an agent monitoring and reflecting on one's experiences and exerting self-influence as in acting on the environment. It is simply a shift in perspective of the same agent between self and environment. Even when individuals are the object of external influence, they are not just passive recipients of stimulus inputs. They act agentically on that influence in cognitive, affective, and behavioral ways that enhance, neutralize or subvert it. Rather than splitting the self into object and agent, social cognitive theory treats this static dichotomy as a dynamic system of interlocking functions.

Social cognitive theory also rejects the fractionation of human agency into multiple selves. A theory of personality cast in terms of multiple selves plunges one into deep philosophical waters. It requires a regress of selves to a presiding overseer self that selects and manages the collection of selves to suit given purposes. Actually, there is only one self that can visualize different futures and select courses of action designed to attain desired futures and avoid aversive ones. Actions are regulated by a person not by a cluster of selves doing the choosing and guiding. The fractionation of agency into different types of selves poses additional conceptual problems.

Diversity of action arises not from a collection of agentive selves but from the different options considered by the one and the same agentive self. It is the person who is doing the thinking, regulating, and reflecting not a homunculus-overseeing self. People striving to realize an envisioned future guide and motivate their efforts through a set of self-regulatory mechanisms. These are governed by appraisal of personal capabilities for different pursuits, long-range aspiration merged with working proximal subgoals that lead to its fulfillment, positive and negative outcome expectations for different life courses, the value placed on those envisioned outcomes, and the perceived environmental constraints and opportunity structures. These represent some of the influential sociocognitive determinants of the courses that lives take. One and the same person exercises these self-influences differentially for different purposes, in different activity domains, and in different social contexts.

Structure of Self System

The affinity to global dispositional constructs has also fostered a disjoined duality of process and structure that pervades the field of personality. This dualistic view is also reflected in the dichotomization of personality theories as embodying structuralism or functionalism. Theories that specify how human agency is exercised are often mistakenly depicted as solely process theories. Trait approaches are said to be structural theories. Social cognitive theory rejects this false separateness of structural and process theories. Regulatory processes operate through guiding self structures rather than disembodied from them.

Self structures do not emerge autonomously and give rise to behavior divorced from any operational processes. Developed self structures are translated into actions through regulatory functions. The experiences produced by regulatory processes operating on the environment, in turn, shape self structures. In short, both the structure of a self system and the regulatory processes must work together in human functioning. To illustrate the interdependence of structure and process consider the self-regulation of moral conduct.

Social cognitive theory provides a detailed account of how moral standards are constructed through cognitive processing of diverse sources of information conveyed by modeled moral commitments, direct instruction in moral precepts, and the evaluative reactions of others to conduct that has ethical and moral significance. The nature and pattern of the acquired moral standards represent an enduring cognitive structure for judging the moral status of conduct in situations containing many morally relevant decisional ingredients. Moral structure is translated into action via self-regulatory mechanisms operating through a set of agentive subfunctions. These include self-monitoring of conduct; judging the conduct in relation to one's moral standards and the circumstances under which it occurs; and applying evaluative self-sanctions depending on whether the conduct measures up to the internal standards or violates them. In short, processes do not operate in a vacuum without structural properties that provide the substance and direction for those processes. People do not run around mindlessly engaging in structure-free processing of experiences.

A social cognitive theory combining moral rule structures and self-regulative processes operating through them is no less a structural theory of personality than, the psychoanalytic approach in which a superego is posited as a structural feature of personality that controls conduct. The major differences between these two theories are in globality of constructs, explicitness of acquisitional and regulative mechanisms, and explanatory and predictive power, not in whether one theory postulates a structure and the other does not. Moral rule structures do not operate as invariant internal regulators of conduct. Selfregulatory mechanisms do not operate unless they are activated, and there are many processes by which self-sanctions can be disengaged from internal standards to perpetrate inhumane conduct. Selective activation and disengagement of internal control thus permits different types of conduct with the same moral standards.

Many inhumanities are perpetrated by people who, in other aspects of their lives and other circumstances, behave in considerate, compassionate ways. Consideration of the conjoint operation of moral rule structures, selfregulatory mechanisms and contextual influences helps to explain this seeming paradox where more global structures alone do not. We shall return to the issue of selective self-regulation later. The nature and regulative function of self-conceptions provides a further illustration in which relinquishment of global measures is sometimes misconstrued as abandonment of structure.

Self-appraisal has traditionally been conceptualized in personality theory in terms of the self-concept. Such self theories are concerned, for the most part, with global self-images.

A global self-conception does not do justice to the multifaceted structure of self-belief systems. They can vary substantially across different life domains and operate dynamically in concert with other psychosocial determinants. Thus, people's self-conceptions as parents may differ from their occupational self-conception and, even in the occupational realm, their self-conceptions are likely to differ for different facets of occupational competency. Composite self-images are not equal to the task of predicting with any degree of accuracy such intraindividual variability.

Social cognitive theory approaches the structure of self-belief systems in more refined, domain-linked ways that have greater explanatory and predictive power. A multifaceted approach does not mean that there is no structure or generality to human functioning. Conversely, life would be exceedingly costly and perilous if people remained blissfully inattentive to situational factors signifying appropriate courses of action and indifferent to the personal and social effects of what they do. In short, neither isolated specificity nor obtuse indiscriminativeness is adaptive.

Trait theorists framed the issue of human adaptiveness in terms of "consistency" with misleading connotations that perpetuated the search for behavioral fixedness. Consistency not only implies virtues of steadfastness and principled conduct, but it sets up the contrast as "inconsistency" implying instability or expediency. In fact, action devoid of discriminative forethought would produce disastrous results. Nevertheless, the inverted value implications diverted attention from analyses of the dynamic nature of human adaptation to an elusive search on how to extract consistency from variability and efforts to explain how the same global disposition can spawn highly variable conduct.

In fact, as already noted, adaptive functioning requires both generalization and differentiation of action. Therefore, social cognitive theory addresses the determinants and mechanisms governing both generality and specificity of action rather than championing only variability. Whether people behave uniformly or variably depends heavily upon the functional equivalence of the environments. Thus, if acting intelligently in diverse settings has functional value, people will be consistently intelligent in situations that otherwise differ markedly. By contrast, if directives to subordinates improve performance but giving commands to bosses brings rebukes, people will behave authoritatively with subordinates but diplomatically with bosses.

Nor is consistency across expressive modalities a blessing. If people acted on every thought that entered their minds, or if their affect ruled every action, they would get themselves into very serious trouble. Here, too, they have to regulate their actions and affective expressions discriminatively. These behavioral signatures of personality are functionally related to conditional influences that facilitate or deter certain styles of behavior. The particular organization of conditional relations characterizes the uniqueness and coherence of personality for any given individual.

Behavior patterns are not necessarily locked in

temporally either. Otherwise, people would not alter their behavior over the course of their development to suit their age and the changing demands of life. Changes over the life course take diverse forms across spheres of functioning rather than follow a consistent, unidirectional course. Whether social behavior is invariant or changes over time depends partly on the degree of continuity of environmental conditions over the time span that affect the functional value of different forms of behavior. However, environments are diverse rather than monolithic. In the agentic constructivist perspective of social cognitive theory, people have a hand in promoting continuities in their life. They do so by selecting environments compatible with their values, attributes, and aspirations and by constructing social environments through their actions.

We are all acquainted with problem-prone individuals who, by their aversive conduct, breed negative social milieus wherever they go. In contrast those skilled in bringing out the best in others create beneficial social milieus. Through selection and construction of environments, personality patterns can become self-perpetuating. Protracted disputes continue to be fought under the banners of the idiographic view that people behave idiosyncratically as though they have no processes in common, or the nomothetic view that people's behavior follows general principles that allegedly grant no individuality. These disputes often fail to distinguish between what one thinks, feels, values and can do from the basic mechanisms by which these personal proclivities are developed and regulated. People obviously differ in their make-up because they come with different biological endowments and experience different admixtures of influences. But cultures provide numerous common direct and modeling influences that create many similar proclivities.

An ideographic psychology solely of uniqueness would be a feeble scientific enterprise devoid of generalizability and operative utility. With regard to mechanisms, all people learn through modeling and the effects of their actions. Indeed, in many cultures the word for "teach" is the same as the word for "show".

People regulate their motivation and actions anticipatorily by judgments of their capabilities, goal aspirations, outcome expectations, and perceived environmental opportunity structures and impediments. Thus, there is diversity in sociostructural arrangements and the forms that lives take in different social milieus but universality in the basic acquisitional and regulative mechanisms. Continuity has meaning when applied to distinct styles of behavior. But it takes on considerable indefiniteness when judged in terms of broad categories of adaptation. One can always find linkages between early and later endeavors as, between pursuit of scholarship in childhood and professional careers in adulthood. However, at this level of generality, continuity can be achieved through a variety of life paths. Personal lives, whether marked by continuities or discontinuities have their particular characters.

The rapid pace of social and technological changes increasingly requires new forms of adaptation throughout the life course. Broad adaptational categories mask personal changes over time. As in the explanation of both generality and specificity of behavior across contextual variations, a comprehensive theory must also explain both temporal continuities and change. The dualistic thinking is also reflected in suggestions that the processes of sociocognitive theories be combined with trait theory, such as the five-factor taxonomy, to form the comprehensive theory of personality.

According to trait structuralists, factor analyses of everyday descriptors of behavior culled from dictionaries and personality questionnaires will yield the supertraits that constitute the basic structure of personality. Some of the trait theorists rallied with missionary zeal around the "Big Five" global supertraits of extraversion, agreeableness, conscientiousness, neuroticism, and openness to experience as the universal features of personality structure. The epistemological issue in that metaphoric armchair, which incidentally has served other scientific disciplines remarkably well, centers on whether personologists or machines do the conceptualizing.

The essentially atheoretical strategy of research, the shrinking of personal characteristics to a few global traits, the empirical status of the extracted traits, and the exaggerated claims of consensuality regarding the fivefold taxonomy drew sharp critiques. Although the fivefold clustering is presented as a "model," a descriptive classification of habitual behavior is not a conceptual model, which must specify a system of postulates governing the phenomenon of interest. Seeking the structure of personality by factor analyzing a limited collection of behavioral descriptors essentially reduces to a psychometric method in search of a theory.

Development of a comprehensive theory of personality requires an integrated conceptual scheme that classifies not only behaviors but specifies their determinants and key mechanisms through which they operate and the modes by which desired ones can be fostered and undesired ones altered. Theory guides the development of appropriate measures, specifies the conditions for empirical verification of its core propositions, and informs effective psychosocial programs of change. The so-called supertraits are essentially clusters of habitual behaviors.

People are asked to rate whether they are courteous, methodical, curious, fearful, get into arguments, and the like. It comes as no surprise, that a collection of behaviors that resemble one another, such as being organized, dutiful, disciplined, and effortful form a behavioral cluster dubbed "conscientiousness." Some of the clusters cohere better than others depending on the degree of redundancy of behavioral descriptors representing them. However, descriptive behavioral clusters tell us little about the determinants and regulative structures governing the behaviors that make up a particular cluster.

In trait analyses, the behavioral descriptors tend to get reified as causes of behavior. Conscientious behavior is said to affect how well people perform on a job. One can, of course, use past conscientious performance as a predictor of future conscientious job performance. But conscientious behavior is neither a personality structure nor is such behavior a cause of itself. The proponents of taxonomies founded on behavioral descriptors locate the personality structure in the wrong place.

The paucity of guiding theory in seeking the structure of personality through factor analyses of behavioral descriptors is further revealed in the ambiguity about the sources of the supertraits. The apparent fixedness of personal attributes throughout adulthood most likely has more to do with the insensitivity of nonconditional global measures than with unchangeableness of personal factors over the life course.

Global measures of personal attributes mask significant patterns of changes with age that domain-linked measures reveal. Adding conditional factors to personality assessments further increases their sensitivity to variability in the way individuals behave in different social contexts.

Each of the supertraits is a conglomerate of facets. The supertrait openness to experience includes such diverse activities as endorsement of day dreaming, rejection of religious authority, excitement over art and poetry, support of controversial speakers, and trying foreign foods. An individual may display high intellectual curiosity and openness to technical and commercial ideas but not care much about exotic foods or what the glitterotti decree is modern art. By contrast, another individual may support diverse artistic endeavors but act like a Luddite toward technological innovations. Efforts to understand the nature, origin, and predictiveness of scientific curiosity, for example, should not clutter the personal determinant with preferences for exotic foods. It is not that a general disposition predicts behavior, but that a few of the behavioral descriptors in the conglomerate mixture may provide some overlap with the particular behavior being predicted to yield a correlate.

Global conglomerates do not lend themselves to causal analyses because human experiences do not occur at the level of averaged behavioral conglomerates or life circumstances reduced to a nondescript average. Nor are conglomerate measures equipped to explain the wide variations in behavior by the same individual in a given domain of activity under different situational circumstances. Trait theorists sought to remedy the weak predictiveness of trait indices by averaging ratings of behavior across situations and occasions, which presumably provides a truer measure of the trait. However, aggregation does not produce much predictive gain when actual behavior in different situations rather than self-reports of behavior is measured. No amount of aggregation will elevate correlations between a given form of behavior under different circumstances that social sanctions have disjoined.

Aggressive acts by delinquents toward parish priests and toward rival gang members will correlate poorly, however much averaging one does. In a world characterized by contingency, one can lose rather than gain predictive power by trying to predict behavior from an average value that typifies neither situation. The situational averaging solution reminds one of the nonswimmer who drowned while crossing a river that averaged only three feet in depth. Other efforts to boost correlates included aggregating differing forms of conduct, such as physical aggression, verbal aggression, and antagonistic conduct into a conglomerate index.

Mixing behaviors obscures the understanding of psychological functioning as does the mixing of situations. To be able to predict through aggregation that individuals will sometime, somewhere, do something within a wide assortment of acts is of no great interest. People want to know whether adolescent offenders are likely to commit physical assaults, not whether sometime, somewhere, they may speak offensively or behave antagonistically, or do something else untoward. There is little evidence that the repackaging of traits in a fivefold format has produced any better prediction of human behavior than do the traditional trait measures, which are not much to rave about.

The inflated self-congratulatory claims of breakthrough stand in stark contrast to the paucity of empirical reality tests of predictiveness. It is the replication of fivefold clustering rather than evidence of predictive power that seems to be racing the pulse of adherents to this taxonomic view of personality. It should be noted in passing that the standard correlate of omnibus trait measures is not as commonly assumed. When it comes to predicting particular forms of behavior, global measures are weaker or nonsignificant predictors. Gains in social consensus among trait theorists about the number of supertraits without gains in predictive power hardly constitutes an advance in the field of personality. Job productivity is often cited as a domain in which the predictive utility of the fivefold approach has been demonstrated. In commenting on behavioral description versus prediction, that the fivefold supertraits are not only too general and heterogeneous in facets but lack relevant factors to be useful in accounting for job performance.

Innumerable studies have shown that personal goals are consistent predictors of job productivity. Even the relationship between conscientiousness and sales performance disappears when the influence of the goals employees set for themselves is removed. Given the view that personality is essentially unchangeable after early adulthood, this taxonomic approach offers little hope of self-betterment along the life course for those who happened to have gotten off to a poor start. Once cast into a nonconscientious mold by innate endowment and experience, one remains ever nonconscientious thereafter. To continue with the productivity example, goal theory offers a much more optimistic view of human changeableness with sound conceptual and empirical backing on how to instill goals and how they work.

Teaching people how to regulate their motivation and activities through goal setting enables them to achieve sizeable increases in productivity regardless of their age or sphere of activity. Except for a relationship between openness to experience and academic achievement, the big five factors proved unpredictive. Social cognitive theory provides explicit guidelines on how to build a resilient sense of efficacy, which adds to the social utility of the theory. Perceived self-efficacy operates in concert with other sociocognitive factors in a multifaceted causal structure.

The addition of goal aspirations, outcome expectations, and perceived opportunities and impediments would further enhance the predictive power of the theory. The value of a psychological theory is judged not only by its explanatory and predictive power but also by its operative power to guide change in human functioning. A descriptive taxonomy of aggregated behaviors offers no guidance on how to effect personal or social change.

Social cognitive theory provides a large body of particularized knowledge on how to develop the cognitive structures and enlist the processes of the self system that govern human adaptation and change. It lends itself readily to applications because the factors it posits are empirically anchored in indices of functioning and are amenable to change. The determinants and mechanisms through which they operate are spelled out so the theory provides explicit guidelines on how to structure conditions that foster personal and social change. One could argue that a taxonomic scheme is not designed to be explanatory or prescriptive for change. However, trait theorists often make conflicting claims.

On the one hand, their classification scheme is portrayed as simply a descriptive taxonomy. Once the major classes of behavior are firmly established, their origins and functions could be examined. On the other hand, behavioral characteristics are often reified as dynamic causal factors. This creates a serious problem of circularity: Behavior becomes the cause of behavior. Even as descriptive taxonomies, global traits cannot shed much light on the nature of personal causation because personal determinants operate conditionally at a particular contextualized level not at a socially detached conglomerate level.

Social Structure and Personal Agency

Human adaptation and change are rooted in social systems. Therefore, personal agency operates within a broad network of sociostructural influences. In these agentic transactions, people are producers as well as products of social systems. Social structures are devised to organize, guide, and regulate human affairs in given domains by authorized rules and sanctions.

For the most part, social structures represent authorized social practices carried out by human beings occupying designated roles. Within the rule structures, there is a lot of personal variation in their interpretation, enforcement, adoption, circumvention, or active opposition. It is not a dichotomy between a disembodied social structure and personal agency but a dynamic interplay between individuals and those who preside over the institutionalised operations of social systems.

Social structures are created by human activity. The

structural practices, in turn, impose constraints and provide resources and opportunity structures for personal development and functioning. Given this dynamic bidirectionality of influence, social cognitive theory rejects a dualism between personal agency and social structure. Sociostructural theories and psychological theories are often regarded as rival conceptions of human behavior or as representing different levels and proximity of causation. Human behavior cannot be fully understood solely in terms of sociostructural factors or psychological factors.

A full understanding requires an integrated perspective in which sociostructural influences operate through psychological mechanisms to produce behavioral effects. However, the self system is not merely a conduit for external influences. The self is socially constituted but, by exercising self-influence, human agency operates generatively and proactively on social systems not just reactively.

In the theory of triadic reciprocal causation, sociostructural and personal determinants are treated as cofactors within a unified causal structure. Diverse lines of research lend support to this interdependent multicausality. For example, poverty is not a matter of multilayered or distal causation. Lacking the money to provide for the subsistence of one's family impinges pervasively on everyday life in a very specific, proximal way.

Elder and his colleagues show that economic hardship, by itself, has no direct influence on parents' efficacy to promote their children's development. Families who feel overwhelmed by the hardships experience high subjective strain, whereas those who feel they can make it through tough times experience less emotional strain. In intact households, subjective strain impairs parental efficacy by increasing marital discord. For single parents, subjective strain weakens parents' sense of efficacy both directly and by creating feelings of despondency. Thus the impact of both economic conditions and family structure operate through self processes.

Similarly, socioeconomic status does not directly affect children's academic development. Rather, it does so by influencing parents' educational aspirations for their children. Parental aspirations and belief in their educational parenting efficacy, in turn, influence their children's scholastic performances by raising their educational aspirations and beliefs in their scholastic capabilities.

Different facets of perceived self-efficacy operating in concert with other psychosocial factors contribute to academic achievement through different mediated paths. Multifaceted measures thus provide a refined view of causal structures that global measures of perceived efficacy cannot provide. A similar integrated causality governs occupational trajectories of youth. Socioeconomic status has no direct effects on either occupational efficacy or career considerations. Rather, it has an indirect impact by influencing parents' beliefs in their efficacy to promote their children's educational development and the aspirations they hold for them. Parental efficacy and aspirations raise children's educational aspirations and their sense of academic, social, and self-regulatory efficacy.

The patterning of children's perceived efficacy influences the types of occupational activities they believe they can do, which, in turn, is linked to the kinds of jobs they would choose for their life's work. In other aspects of family functioning, the impact of socioeconomic status on child outcomes is entirely mediated through parents' child management practices. Similar paths of multicausality mediated through self processes are evident in the functioning of educational systems as well as familial systems. Schools that have many poor students and those of disadvantaged minority status generally do poorly academically. However, these sociodemographic characteristics exert their impact on schools' level of achievement largely by shaping teachers' beliefs in their collective efficacy to motivate and educate their students. Schools that have teachers who believe strongly in their collective instructional efficacy do well academically regardless of the sociodemographic characteristics of the student bodies. In verifying the path of influence from sociostructural conditions through familial and self-regulatory processes, these types of studies clarify how personal agency operates within a broad network of sociostructural influences.

Fundamental Capabilities

In social cognitive theory, people are neither driven by global traits nor automatically shaped and controlled by the environment. They function as contributors to their own motivation, behavior, and development within a network of reciprocally interacting influences. Persons are characterized within this theoretical perspective in terms of a number of fundamental capabilities. These are reviewed in the sections that follow.

Symbolizing capability: Social cognitive theory assigns a central role to cognitive, vicarious, self-regulatory, and self-reflective processes in human development and functioning. The extraordinary capacity to represent events and their relationships in symbolic form provides humans with a powerful tool for comprehending their environment and for creating and managing environmental conditions that touch virtually every aspect of their lives. Symbols serve as the vehicle of thought.

Most environmental events exert their effects through cognitive processing rather than directly. Cognitive factors partly determine which environmental events are observed, what meaning is conferred on them, what emotional impact and motivating power they have, and how the information they convey is organized and preserved for future use. Through the medium of symbols, people transform transient experiences into cognitive models that serve as guides for reasoning and action. People transcend time and place in communicating with others at any distance. By symbolizing their experiences, people give structure, meaning, and continuity to their lives.

Knowledge provides the substance and thinking operations provide the tools for cognitive problem solving. Rather than solve problems solely by performing actions and suffering the consequences of missteps, people usually test possible solutions in thought. They generate alternative solutions to problems, and discard or retain them based on estimated outcomes without having to go through a laborious behavioral search. The remarkable flexibility of symbolization also enables people to create novel and fanciful ideas that transcend their sensory experiences. One can easily think of cows jumping over the moon even though these feats are physically impossible. The other distinctive human capabilities are founded on this advanced capacity for symbolization. However, in keeping with the interactional perspective, social cognitive theory specifies the social origins of thought and the mechanisms through which social factors exert their influence on cognitive functioning. Although the capacity for symbolization vastly expands human capabilities, if put to faulty use, it can also breed personal distress.

Many human dysfunctions and torments stem from problems of thought. This is because, in their thoughts, people often dwell on painful pasts and on perturbing futures of their own invention. They burden themselves with stressful arousal through anxiety-provoking rumination. They debilitate their own efforts by self-doubting and other self-defeating ideation. They constrain and impoverish their lives through phobic thinking. They drive themselves to despondency by harsh self-evaluation and dejecting modes of thinking. And they often act on misconceptions that get them into trouble. Thought can thus be a source of human failings and distress as well as a source of human accomplishments.

Vicarious capability: A comprehensive theory of personality must explain the acquisition of competencies, attitudes, values, and emotional proclivities not just the enactments of behaviors that get dubbed as traits. There are two basic modes of learning. People learn by experiencing the effects of their actions and through the power of social modeling. Psychological theories have focused almost exclusively on learning from positive and negative response consequences.

Natural endowment provides humans with enabling biological systems but few inborn skills. They must be developed over long periods and altered to fit changing conditions over the life course. If knowledge and skills had to be shaped laboriously by response consequences without the benefit of modeled guidance, a culture could never transmit its language, social practices, mores, and adaptive competencies. Mistakes can produce costly or even fatal consequences. The prospects of survival would, therefore, be slim indeed if one had to rely solely on trial-and-error experiences.

Moreover, the constraints of time, resources, and mobility impose severe limits on the situations and activities that can be directly explored for the acquisition of new knowledge and skills. Fortunately, the tedious and hazardous trial-and-error learning can be short cut by social modeling. Humans have evolved an advanced capacity for observational learning that enables them to expand their knowledge and competencies rapidly through the information conveyed by the rich variety of models.

Virtually all behavioral, cognitive, and affective learning from direct experience can be achieved vicariously by observing people's actions and the consequences for them. Much human learning occurs either designedly or unintentionally from the models in one's immediate environment. However, a vast amount of knowledge about people, places, and styles of thinking and behaving is gained from the extensive modeling in the symbolic environment of the electronic mass media.

A major significance of symbolic modeling lies in its tremendous scope and multiplicative power. Unlike learning by doing, which requires shaping the actions of each individual through repeated consequences, in observational learning a single model can transmit new ways of thinking and behaving simultaneously to many people in widely dispersed locales. Video and computer delivery systems feeding off telecommunications satellites are now rapidly diffusing new ideas, values, and styles of conduct worldwide.

Most psychological theories were cast long before the advent of revolutionary advances in the technology of communication. As a result, they give insufficient attention to the increasingly powerful role that the symbolic environment plays in contemporary societies. Television has vastly expanded the range of models to which members of society are exposed day in and day out.

By drawing on these modeled patterns of thought and behaviour, observers transcend the bounds of their immediate environment. Because the symbolic environment occupies a major part of people's everyday lives, the study of human development and acculturation in the electronic era must be broadened to include electronic acculturation. At the societal level, symbolic modes of modeling are transforming how social systems operate and serving as a major vehicle for sociopolitical change.

Observational learning, which can take the form of behavioral, cognitive, valuational, and affective change, is governed by four component subfunctions.

— *Attentional processes determine* what people observe in the profusion of modeling influences and what information they extract from what they notice. People cannot be much influenced by observed events if they do not remember them.

— *Governing observational learning concerns representational processes.* Retention involves an active process of transforming and restructuring the information conveyed by modeled events into rules and conceptions for memory representation.

— *The behavioral production process-symbolic conceptions are translated into appropriate courses of action.* This is achieved through a conception-matching process in which behavioral enactments are structured until they match the conception of the activity. Behavior operates under hierarchical levels of control. Cognitive guidance is important in early and intermediate phases of competency development. Once proficient modes of behavior become routinized, they are regulated largely by lower sensory-motor systems and no longer require higher cognitive control. However, when routinized behavior patterns fail to produce desired results, cognitive control again comes into play in the search for better solutions. Control reverts to lower control systems after an adequate means is found and becomes the habitual way of doing things. Partial disengagement of thought from proficient action has considerable functional value because it frees cognitive activity for matters requiring attention. If one had to think before carrying out every routine activity, it would consume most of one's attention and create a monotonously dull inner life. Efficient functioning requires a mix of routinized and mindful action. As a result of routinization, people often react with fixed ways of thinking unreflectively and with habitual ways of behaving unthinkingly. Nonconscious information processing and routinization of thought and action should be distinguished from an unconscious mind acting as a concealed agent orchestrating behavior in an unwitting host organism. To reify, from evidence of automatic and routinized responses, a subterranean agent steering perceptions and actions is to commit a serious metaphysical transgression.

— *Modeling concerns motivational processes:* Social cognitive theory distinguishes between acquisition and performance because people do not perform everything they learn. Performance of observationally learned behavior is influenced by three major types of incentive motivators-direct, vicarious, and self-produced. People are more likely to adopt modeled styles of behavior if they produce valued outcomes than if they have unrewarding or punishing effects.

The observed cost and benefits accruing to others influence the adoption of modeled patterns in much the same way as do directly experienced consequences. People are motivated by the successes of others who are similar to themselves, but they are discouraged from pursuing courses of behavior that they have seen often result in aversive consequences. The evaluative reactions people generate to their own behavior also regulate which observationally learned activities they are most likely to pursue. People express what they find self-satisfying and reject what they personally disapprove.

Forethought capability: Another distinctive human characteristic is the capacity for forethought. The ability to bring anticipated outcomes to bear on current activities promotes foresightful behavior. It enables people to transcend the dictates of their immediate environment and to shape and regulate the present to fit a desired future. Much human self-directedness is the product of forethought.

The future time perspective manifests itself in many different ways. People set goals for themselves, anticipate the likely consequences of prospective actions, and plan courses of action likely to produce desired outcomes and avoid detrimental ones. Through the exercise of forethought, people motivate themselves and guide their actions anticipatorily.

As people progress in their life course they continue to plan ahead, reorder their priorities, and structure their lives accordingly. The capacity for intentional purposive action is rooted in symbolic activity. Future events cannot, of course, be causes of current motivation and action because they have no actual existence.

However, by being represented cognitively in the present, foreseeable future events are converted into current motivators and regulators of behavior. In this form of anticipatory selfguidance, behavior is motivated and directed by anticipated outcomes rather than being pulled by an unrealized future state.

Behavioural Outcomes

People regulate their behavior partly by outcome expectations. Courses of action that are likely to produce positive outcomes are generally adapted and used; those that bring unrewarding or punishing outcomes are usually discarded. Response consequences do not automatically shape and control actions as claimed by radical behaviorists. Rather, people construct outcome expectations from observed conditional relations between environmental events and between given actions and outcomes.

In social cognitive theory, "reinforcement" is a form of incentive motivation operating through outcome expectations rather than an automatic strengthener of responses. Because outcomes exert their influence through forethought, they have little or no motivational or behavioral impact until people discover how outcomes are linked to actions in their environment. This is no easy matter. In everyday life, actions usually produce mixed effects:

> The outcomes may occur immediately or far removed in time; the same behavior may have different effects depending on where, when, and toward whom it is performed, and many situational factors affect behavioral outcomes. Such causal ambiguity provides a fertile ground for misjudgment. When belief about the effects of actions differs from actuality, behavior is weakly controlled by its actual consequences until repeated experience instills realistic beliefs. Yet it is not always one's beliefs that change in the direction of social reality. Acting on erroneous beliefs can alter how others behave, thus shaping the social reality in the direction of the misbeliefs.

External consequences are not the only kind of outcomes that influence human behavior. People profit from the successes and mistakes of others as well as from their own experiences. As a general rule, they do things they have seen succeed and avoid those they have seen fail. However, observed outcomes exert their influence through perceived similarity that one is likely to experience similar outcomes for similar courses of action and that one possesses the capabilities to achieve similar performances. Observed outcomes can also affect the level of motivation by altering the value of external outcomes through social comparison processes. People weigh their own outcomes by those accruing to others for similar performances. The same monetary raise is likely to be viewed negatively by persons who have seen colleagues compensated more generously, but viewed positively if colleagues have been compensated less well. The relational properties of incentives affect not only motivation and performance but personal satisfaction and discontent. Equitable outcomes foster a sense of well-being; inequitable ones breed discontent and resentment.

Self-regulatory capability: People are not only knowers and performers guided by outcome expectations. They are also self-reactors with a capacity for self-direction. This capability is grounded in a selfregulatory structure. Successful development requires the substitution of internal regulation and direction for external sanctions and demands. Once the capability for self-direction is developed, self-demands and self-sanctions serve as major guides, motivators, and deterrents. In the absence of internal standards and self-sanctions, people would behave like weather vanes, constantly shifting direction to conform to whatever momentary influence happened to impinge upon them.

People cannot influence their own motivation and actions very well if they do not pay adequate attention to their thought processes and performances, the conditions under which they occur, and to the immediate and distal effects they produce. Therefore, success in self-regulation partly depends on the fidelity, consistency, and temporal proximity of self-monitoring. Depending on people's values and the functional significance of different activities, they attend selectively to certain aspects of their functioning and ignore those that are of little import to them. Observing one's pattern of behavior is the first step toward doing something to affect it, but in itself, such information provides little basis for self-directed reactions. Actions give rise to self-reactions through a judgmental function that includes several subsidiary processes. Personal standards for judging and guiding one's actions play a major role in self-motivation and in the exercise of self-directedness. Whether a given performance is regarded favorably or negatively will depend upon the personal standards against which it is evaluated. Once people commit themselves to a valued goal, they seek self-satisfaction from fulfilling it and are prompted to intensify their efforts by discontent with substandard performances.

The anticipated affective self-reactions serve as incentive motivators for personal accomplishments. For most activities, there are no absolute measures of adequacy. People must, therefore, evaluate their performances in relation to the attainments of others. The referential comparisons may take the form of performance attainments of others in similar situations, standard norms based on representative groups, one's own past attainments, or comparative group performance in societies organized around collectivistic principles.

Another factor in the judgmental component of self-regulation concerns the valuation of activities. The more relevant performances are to one's value preferences and sense of personal adequacy, the more likely selfevaluative reactions are to be elicited in that activity. Self-reactions also vary depending on how people perceive the determinants of their behavior. They are most likely to take pride in their accomplishments when they ascribe their successes to their own abilities and efforts. They respond self-critically to faulty performances for which they hold themselves responsible but not to those they perceive as due to unusual circumstances, to insufficient capabilities, or to unrealistic demands.

Motivation based on personal standards involves a cognitive comparison process between the standards and perceived performance attainments. The motivational effects do not stem from the standards themselves but rather from several self-reactive influences. These include perceived self-efficacy to fulfill one's standards, affective self-evaluation of one's attainments, and adjustment of proximal subgoals depending on the progress one is making.

Performance judgments set the occasion for self-reactive influence. Self-reactions provide the linking mechanism by which standards regulate courses of action. The self-regulatory control is achieved by creating incentives for one's own actions and by anticipative affective reactions to one's own behavior depending on how it measures up to personal standards. Thus, people pursue courses of action that give them self-satisfaction and a sense of self-worth, but they refrain from behaving in ways that result in self-censure. Some of the self-motivating incentives may be tangible outcomes, as when people get themselves to do things they would otherwise put off or avoid altogether by making tangible rewards dependent upon performance attainments. However, people value their self-respect and the self-satisfaction derived from a job well done more highly than they do material rewards. The self-regulation of behavior by self-evaluative reactions is a uniquely human capability. Selfevaluation gives direction to behavior and creates motivators for it.

Most theories of self-regulation are founded on a negative feedback system. In this view, negative discrepancy between one's perceived performance and an adopted standard motivates action to reduce the disparity. However, self-regulation by negative discrepancy tells only half the story and not necessarily the more interesting half. People are proactive, aspiring organisms. Human self-motivation relies both on discrepancy production and discrepancy reduction. It requires proactive control as well as reactive control.

People initially motivate themselves through proactive control by setting themselves valued performance standards that create a state of disequilibrium and then mobilizing their effort on the basis of anticipatory estimation of what it would take to reach them. Feedback control comes into play in subsequent adjustments of effort expenditure to achieve desired results. After people attain the standard they have been pursuing, those who have a strong sense of efficacy generally set a higher standard for themselves. The adoption of further challenges creates new motivating discrepancies to be mastered.

After self-regulatory capabilities are developed, behavior usually produces two sets of consequences: self-evaluative reactions and external outcomes. They may operate as complementary or opposing influences on behavior. External outcomes are most likely to wield influence when they are compatible with self-evaluative ones. This condition exists when externally rewardable actions are a source of self-satisfaction and self-pride and when externally punishable ones bring self-censure. Behavior is also highly susceptible to external influences in the absence of countervailing internal standards. People with weak commitment to personal standards adopt a pragmatic orientation, tailoring their behavior to fit whatever the situation seems to call for. They become adept at reading social cues and varying their self-presentation accordingly.

People commonly experience conflicts of outcomes when they are rewarded socially or materially for behavior they personally devalue. When self-devaluative consequences outweigh the force of external rewards they have little sway. There is no more devastating consequence than self-contempt. But if the allure of rewards outweigh self-censure, the result can be cheerless compliance. However, people possess sociocognitive skills for reconciling perturbing disparities between personal standards and conduct. The mechanisms by which losses of self-respect for devalued conduct are reduced is considered shortly.

Another type of conflict of outcomes arises when individuals are punished for activities they value highly. Principled dissenters and nonconformists often find themselves in such predicaments. The relative strength of self-approval and external censure determine whether the courses of action will be pursued or abandoned. There are individuals, however, whose sense of self-worth is so strongly invested in certain convictions that they will submit to prolonged maltreatment rather than accede to what they regard as unjust or immoral. Another common situation is one in which both the external support and reward for given activities are minimal or lacking, and individuals have to sustain their efforts largely through self-encouragement. Innovators persevere despite repeated failures in endeavors that provide neither rewards nor recognition for long periods, if at all during their lifetime. Innovative pursuits that clash with existing preferences bring criticism and social rejection. To persist, innovators must be sufficiently convinced of their efficacy, the worth of their pursuit to self-reward their efforts, and not be much concerned with the opinions of others.

Self-Regulation

The accelerated pace of social and technological changes has placed a premium on people's capabilities to exert a strong hand in their own development and functioning through the life course. Information technologies are transforming the educational system. In the past, students have had to rely heavily on classroom teachers for their knowledge. Students now have the best libraries, museums and multimedia instruction at their fingertips through the global Internet for educating themselves. Efficacious self-regulators gain knowledge, skills and intrinsic interests in intellectual matters. Weak selfregulators do not achieve much progress in self-development. The recent years have witnessed a major change in the conception of health from a disease model to a health model. Viewed from this perspective, human health is heavily dependent on lifestyle habits and environmental conditions. It emphasizes health enhancement not just disease prevention. By exercising control over health habits, people can live longer and healthier.

New health promotion systems structured around self-regulatory principles are reducing major health risks, slowing the rate of biological aging and enhancing health. Self-regulation is also becoming a key factor in occupational life. In the past, employees learned a given trade and performed it much the same way during their lifetime in the same organization. Much of the world of work is now being structured so that employees assume operational control in flexible self-managed teams. In the modern workplace, knowledge and technical skills are quickly outmoded unless they are updated to fit the new technologies. Employees have to take charge of their self-development over the full course of their worklife. Efficacious innovativeness and adaptability has become a premium at the organizational level as well. These new realities place increasing demands on individual and collective efficacy to shape personal destinies and the national life of societies.

A favorable self-regulatory system provides a continuing source of motivation, selfdirectedness and personal satisfaction. However, a dysfunctional self system can also breed much human misery. For people who adopt stringent personal standards, most of their accomplishments bring them a sense of failure and self-disparagement. In its more extreme forms, harsh standards of self-evaluation give rise to despondency, chronic discouragement, feelings of worthlessness and lack of purposefulness. Effective treatments must remedy each of the dysfunctional aspects of the self-system. They correct selfbelittling interpretative biases, promote adoption of attainable subgoals that provide a sense of accomplishment, and get clients to be more self-rewarding. High aspirations do not produce self-demoralization as long as current attainments are measured against attainable subgoals of progress rather than in terms of lofty ultimate goals.

Self-Reflectiveness

The process of thought verification involves comparing how well one's thoughts match some indicator of reality. There are four modes of thought verification: enactive, vicarious, persuasory, and logical. Enactive verification relies on the closeness of the fit between one's thoughts and the results of the actions they spawn. Good matches lend validity to the thoughts; mismatches refute them. In the vicarious mode of thought verification, seeing the effects of other people's actions provides the check on the correctness of one's own thinking. Vicarious thought verification is not simply a supplement to enactive validation. Symbolic modeling vastly expands the range of verification experiences that cannot be attained by personal action because of the constraints of time, resources, and mobility. Some spheres of life involve highly specialized knowledge requiring dependence on experts or metaphysical ideas that are not amenable to empirical confirmation. When experiential verification is difficult or unfeasible, people evaluate the soundness of their views by checking them with what others, to whom they give credence, believe. Thoughts are also verified by inferential means.

In logical verification, people can check for fallacies in their thinking by deducing from knowledge that is known and what necessarily follows from it. Such metacognitive activities usually foster dependable thought, but they can produce faulty thought patterns as well. Forceful actions arising from erroneous beliefs often create social environments that confirm the misbeliefs. Verification of thought by comparison with distorted media versions of social reality can foster shared misconceptions of people, places, or things. Social verification can foster bizarre views of reality if the shared beliefs of the reference group with which one affiliates are eccentric and the group is encapsulated from outside social ties and influences. Similarly, deductive reasoning will be flawed if the propositional knowledge on which it is based is faulty or biases intrude on reasoning processes.

Self Efficacy

Among the self-referent thoughts that influence human motivation, affect and action, none is more central or pervasive than people's judgments of the personal efficacy. Perceived self-efficacy is concerned with people's beliefs in their capabilities to perform in ways that give them some control over events that affect their lives. Efficacy beliefs form the foundation of human agency. Unless people believe that they can produce desired results by their actions, they have little incentive to act or to persevere in the face of difficulties.

Self-efficacy beliefs are constructed from four principal sources of information. The most authentic and influential source is mastery experiences. This can be achieved by tackling problems in successive attainable steps. Successes build a robust belief in one's efficacy. Failures undermine it, especially in earlier phases of self-development. Moreover, if people have only easy successes, they are readily discouraged by failure or setbacks. Development of resilient selfefficacy requires experiences in overcoming obstacles through perseverant effort.

The second way of creating and strengthening beliefs of personal efficacy is through vicarious experiences. If people see others like themselves succeed by sustained effort, they come to believe that they, too, have the capacity to succeed. Conversely, observing the failures of others instills doubts about one's own ability to master similar activities. Competent models also build efficacy by conveying knowledge and skills for managing environmental demands. Social persuasion is the third way of strengthening people's beliefs in their efficacy. If people are persuaded that they have what it takes to succeed, they exert more effort and are more perseverant than if they harbor self-doubts and dwell on personal deficiencies when problems arise. But effective social persuaders do more than convey faith in people's capabilities. They arrange activities for others in ways that bring success and avoid placing people prematurely in situations where they are likely to fail. People also rely on their physical and emotional states to judge their capabilities. They read their tension, anxiety and depression as signs of personal deficiency.

In activities that require strength and stamina, they interpret fatigue, windedness, and aches and pains as indictors of low physical efficacy. Thus, the fourth way of altering efficacy beliefs is to enhance physical status, reduce negative emotional states and correct misinterpretations of somatic sources of information.

Information that is relevant for judging personal efficacy is not inherently informative. It is only raw data. Experiences become informative through cognitive processing of efficacy information and self-reflective thought. The information conveyed by events must be distinguished from how that information is selected, weighted and integrated into self-efficacy judgments. A host of factors, including personal, social, and situational ones affect how experiences are interpreted. The cognitive processing of efficacy information involves two separate functions. The first is the types of information people attend to and use as indicators of personal efficacy. Sociocognitive theory specifies the set of efficacy indicators that are distinctive for each of the four major modalities of influence.

Beliefs of personal efficacy regulate human functioning through four major processes. They include cognitive, motivational, emotional, and choice processes. The cognitive pathway takes a variety of forms. A major function of thought is to enable people to predict events and to exercise control over those that are important to them. People of high perceived efficacy show greater cognitive resourcefulness, strategic flexibility, and effectiveness in managing their environment. They also set cognized challenges for themselves and visualize success scenarios that provide positive guides for performance. Those who doubt their efficacy visualize failure scenarios that undermine performances by dwelling on things that can go wrong. In appraising situations, people who are assured in their efficacy focus on the opportunities worth pursuing rather than dwell on risks. They take a future time perspective in structuring their lives. Efficacy beliefs play a central role in the self-regulation of motivation.

Most human motivation is cognitively generated. There are three forms of cognitive motivators, around which different theories have been built. These include causal attributions, outcome expectancies, and cognized goals. The corresponding theories are attribution theory, expectancyvalue theory and goal theory. Efficacy beliefs play a key role in each of these motivational systems. The causal attributions people make for their performances affect their motivation. Efficacy beliefs influence causal attributions, regardless of whether the activities involve cognitive attainments, interpersonal transactions, physical performances, or management of health habits. People who regard themselves as highly efficacious ascribe their failures to insufficient effort, inadequate strategies or unfavorable circumstances. Those of low efficacy attribute their failures to low ability.

The effects of causal attributions on achievement strivings are mediated almost entirely through efficacy beliefs. However, there are many activities that, if done well, produce valued outcomes, but they are not pursued by people who doubt they can do what it takes to succeed. Such exclusions of large classes of options are made rapidly on efficacy grounds with little thought of costs and benefits. Rational models of decision making that exclude efficacy judgment sacrifice explanatory and predictive power. Perceived self-efficacy not only sets the slate of options for consideration, but also regulates their implementation. Making decisions in no way ensures that the needed courses of action will be executed successfully, especially in the face of difficulties.

A psychology of decision making requires a psychology of action grounded in enabling and sustaining efficacy beliefs. The capacity to exercise self-influence by personal challenge through goal setting and evaluative reaction to one's own performances provides another major cognitive mechanism of motivation and self-directedness. Efficacy beliefs play a key role in this form of cognitive motivation as well. It is partly on the basis of efficacy beliefs that people choose which goal challenges to undertake, how much effort to invest and how long to persevere in the face of difficulties. When faced with obstacles, setbacks, and failures, those who doubt their abilities slacken their efforts, give up or settle for mediocre solutions. In short, people of high perceived efficacy set motivating goals for themselves, expect their efforts to produce favorable outcomes, ascribe failures to factors that are potentially controllable through ingenuity and effort, view obstacles as surmountable.

People's beliefs in their coping efficacy affect how much stress, anxiety, and depression they experience in threatening or taxing situations. There are four major ways in which efficacy beliefs regulate emotional states. They do so by influencing how threats are cognitively processed, by supporting coping actions that alter the threats, by exercising control over perturbing thought patterns and by alleviating aversive affective states. Efficacy beliefs influence how threats and taxing demands are perceived and cognitively processed. People who believe they can manage threats and adversities view them as less inimical and are not distressed by them. Those who believe they cannot control them experience high anxiety, dwell on their coping deficiencies, view many aspects of their environment as fraught with danger, magnify possible risks and worry about perils that rarely happen. By such thinking, they distress themselves and impair their functioning.

People who have a high sense of coping efficacy lower their stress and anxiety by acting in ways that transform threatening environments into benign ones. The stronger the sense of efficacy, the bolder people are in tackling the problems that breed stress and anxiety and the greater is their success in shaping the environment to their liking. People have to live with a psychic environment that is largely of their own making. Many human distresses result from failures to control disturbing, ruminative thoughts. Control of one's thought processes is, therefore, a key factor in self-regulation of emotional states. In addition, people can exercise control over their affective states by palliative means without altering the causes of their emotional arousal. They do things that bring relief from unpleasant emotional states when these arise. Belief that one can relieve unpleasant emotional states makes them less aversive.

Perceived inefficacy to control things one values also produces depression in varied ways. One route is through unfulfilled aspirations. People who impose on themselves standards of selfworth they judge they cannot attain drive themselves to depression. Depression, in turn, weakens people's beliefs in their own efficacy, creating a downward cycle. A second route to depression is through a low sense of social efficacy to develop social relationships that bring satisfaction to one's life and make chronic stressors easier to bear. A low sense of social efficacy contributes to depression both directly and by curtailing development of social supports. Perceived efficacy and social support operate bidirectionally in human adaptation and change. Supportive relationships, in turn, can enhance personal efficacy. Indeed, social support has beneficial effects only to the extent that it raises perceived coping efficacy. The third route to depression is through thought control efficacy. Much human depression is cognitively generated by dejecting, ruminative thought. A low sense of efficacy to control ruminative thought contributes to the occurrence, duration, and recurrence of depressive episodes.

So far, the analysis of pathways of influence has focused on how efficacy beliefs enable people to create beneficial environments and to exercise control over them. People are partly the product of their environment. By choosing their environments, they can have a hand in what they become. Beliefs of personal efficacy can, therefore, play a key role in shaping the courses lives take by influencing the types of activities and environments people choose to get into. In self-development through choice processes, destinies are shaped by selection of environments known to cultivate valued potentialities and lifestyles. To sum up, people with a low sense of efficacy avoid difficult tasks, which they view as threats. They have low aspirations and weak commitment to the goals they choose to pursue. They turn inward on their self-doubts instead of thinking about how to perform successfully under pressure. When faced with difficulties, they dwell on obstacles, the negative consequences of failure and their personal deficiencies.

Failure makes them lose faith in themselves because they take it as evidence of their inherent incapability. They slacken their efforts or give up quickly in the face of obstacles. They are slow to recover their sense of efficacy after failures or setbacks and easily fall victim to stress and depression. People with high perceived self-efficacy, by contrast, approach difficult tasks as challenges to be mastered rather than threats to be avoided. They develop interest in what they do, set challenges for themselves, and sustain strong commitments to them. They concentrate on how to perform successfully rather than on themselves and disruptive personal concerns when they encounter problems. They attribute their failures to lack of knowledge or skill, faulty strategies, or insufficient effort, all of which are remediable. They redouble their efforts in the face of obstacles and soon recover their self-assurance after setbacks. This outlook sustains motivation, reduces stress, and lowers vulnerability to depression That self-efficacy beliefs yield functional dividends is amply documented by metaanalyses centered on different spheres of functioning. Because social cognitive theory articulates the ways in which a strong sense of efficacy can be instilled and delineates the operative mechanisms, this knowledge has been extensively applied to enhance human functioning in diverse spheres of life. These wide-ranging applications include education, health, psychopathology, athletics, organizational innovations and large-scale social change.

Forms of Human Agency

The exercise of human agency can take different forms. It includes production of effects through direct personal agency; through proxy agency relying on the efforts of intermediaries; and by collective agency, operating through shared beliefs of efficacy, pooled understandings, group aspirations and incentive systems, and collective action. Each of these expressions of agency is rooted in belief in the power to make things happen.

Proxy agency: The preceding analyses addressed the direct exercise of personal agency. In many spheres of life, people do not have direct control over social conditions and institutional practices that affect their lives. Under these circumstances, they seek their well-being and security through the exercise of proxy agency rather than through direct control. In this socially mediated mode of agency, people try to get those who wield influence and power to act on their behalf to get what they want. Moreover, people often turn to proxy control in areas in which they can exert direct influence because they have not developed the means to do so, they believe others can do it better, or they do not want to saddle themselves with some of the burdensome aspects of direct control. Personal control is neither universally desired nor universally exercised as is commonly assumed. There is an onerous side to direct personal control that can dull the appetite for it. The exercise of control requires mastery of knowledge and skills attainable only through long hours of arduous work. Moreover, maintaining proficiency under ever changing conditions of life demands continued investment of time, effort and resources.

Collective agency : Conceptions of human agency have been confined to individual agency. However, people do not live their lives as isolates. They work together to produce the outcomes they desire but cannot accomplish on their own. Social cognitive theory, therefore, extends the conception of mechanisms of human agency to collective agency. People's shared beliefs in their collective power to produce desired outcomes is a crucial ingredient of collective agency. Group performance is the product of interactive and coordinative dynamics of its members. Therefore, perceived collective efficacy is not simply the sum of the efficacy beliefs of individual members. Rather, it is an emergent group-level property. A group, of course, operates through the behavior of its members. It is people acting collectively on a shared belief not a disembodied group mind that is doing the cognizing, aspiring, motivating, and regulating. Personal and collective efficacy differ in the unit of agency, but in both forms, efficacy beliefs serve similar functions and operate through similar processes. The stronger the beliefs people hold about their collective capabilities, the more they achieve.

The patterning of perceived collective political efficacy and trust in the governmental system predicts the form and level of political participation and social activism. People who believe that they can achieve desired changes through citizen action and regard their governmental system as trustworthy and socially responsive display high involvement in conventional models of political action.

In contrast, those who believe they can produce political change through tenacious collective action but view the governmental systems and its leaders a fundamentally unresponsive and untrustworthy favor more confrontive and coercive tactics outside the traditional political channels. The politically apathetic have a low sense of efficacy that they can influence governmental functioning through collective initiatives and are disaffected from the political system as not acting in their interest.

Some people live their lives in individualistically oriented social systems, whereas others do so in collectivistically oriented systems. Some writers inappropriately equate self-efficacy with individualism and pit it against collectivism. In fact, a high sense of personal efficacy contributes just as importantly to group-directedness as to selfdirectedness. If people are to work together successfully, the members of a group have to perform their roles with a high sense of efficacy.

Personal efficacy is valued, not because of reverence for individualism, but because a strong sense of efficacy is vital for successful functioning regardless of whether it is achieved individually or by group members working together. Cross-cultural research on organizational functioning corroborates the universal functional value of efficacy beliefs. Beliefs of personal efficacy contribute to productivity by members of collectivist cultures just as they do by those raised in individualistic cultures. But cultural context shapes how efficacy beliefs are developed, the purposes to which they are put, and the social arrangements through which they are best expressed.

Cultures are not static, uniform entities as the stereotypic portrayals would lead one to believe. Collectivistic systems, founded on Confucianism, Buddhism, or Marxism favor a communal ethic, but they differ from each other in the values, meanings, and customs they promote. There is substantial heterogeneity among individuals in communality within both individualistic and collectivistic cultures and even greater intraindividual variation in communality across social relationships with family members, friends, and colleagues. There are generational and socioeconomic variations in collectivistic cultures with younger and more affluent members adopting more individualistic orientations. Moreover, people express their cultural orientations conditionally rather than invariantly depending on incentive conditions. There are collectivists in individualistic cultures, and individualists in collectivistic cultures. Regardless of cultural background, people achieve the greatest personal efficacy and productivity when their personal orientation is congruent with the social system. Thus, American collectivists do better under a group-oriented system, Chinese individualists do better under an individually oriented system.

The personal orientation rather than the cultural orientation is a major carrier of the effects. Both at the societal and individual level of analysis, a strong perceived efficacy fosters high group effort and performance attainments. Cultures are no longer insular. Global market forces are restructuring national economies and shaping the political and social life of societies. Advanced telecommunications technologies are disseminating ideas, values and styles of behavior transnationally at an unprecedented rate. These new realities call for broadening the scope of cross-cultural analyses beyond the focus on social forces operating within the boundaries of given societies to the forces impinging upon them from abroad. With growing international imbeddedness and interdependence of societies, the issues of interest center on how national and global forces interact to shape the nature of cultural life.

Efficacious Collective Effort in Changing World

Life in the societies of today is increasingly shaped by transnational interdependencies. Because of extensive global interconnectedness, what happens economically and politically in one part of the world can affect the welfare of vast populations elsewhere. The transnational forces, which are hard to disentangle let alone control, challenge the efficacy of governmental systems to exert a determining influence on their own economic and national life. As the need for efficacious collective effort grows, so does the sense of collective powerlessness. Many of the contemporary conditions of life undermine the development of collective efficacy. Some of the transnational market forces may erode or undermine valued cultural aspects of life when they are disregarded or considered detractors from profitability.

Social bonds and common commitments that lack marketability are especially vulnerable to erosion by global market forces. There are no handy social mechanisms or global agencies through which people can shape and regulate transnational practices that affect their lives. As nations wrestle with the loss of control, the public expresses disillusionment and cynicism over whether their leaders and institutions can work for them to improve their lives. Under the new realities of growing transnational control, nation states increase their controlling leverage by merging into larger regional units such as the European Union. Other regional nation states will similarly be forced to merge into larger blocks, otherwise they will have little bargaining power in transnational relations. These regional marriages do not come without a price. Paradoxically, to gain international control, nations have to negotiate reciprocal pacts that require some loss of national autonomy and changes in traditional ways of life.

Some sectors of the society gain from the pacts, other lose. Modern life is increasingly regulated by complex technologies that most people neither understand nor believe they can do much to influence. The very technologies that people create to control their life environment can become a constraining force that, in turn, controls how they think and behave. The social machinery of society is no less challenging. Bureaucracies thwart effective social action. Many of the bureaucratic practices are designed more to benefit the people who run the social systems than to serve the public. Social change does not come easily because beneficiaries build their privileges into protective institutional structures and processes. Those who exercise authority and control wield their power to maintain their advantages. Long delays between action and noticeable results discourage efforts at change. Social efforts to change lives for the better require merging diverse self-interests in support of common core values and goals. Disagreements among different constituencies create additional obstacles to successful collective action. The recent years have witnessed growing social fragmentation into separate interest groups, each exercising its own power. Pluralism is taking the form of antagonistic factionalism. In addition, mass migration of people fleeing tyranny or seeking a better life is changing cultural landscapes. Societies are thus becoming more diverse and harder to unite around a national vision and purpose.

The magnitude of human problems also undermines perceived efficacy to find effective solutions for them. Profound global changes, arising from burgeoning populations, deforestation, desertification of croplands, ozone depletion, and rapid extinction of species by razing their habitats are destroying the intertwined ecosystems that sustain life. Worldwide problems of growing magnitude instill a sense of paralysis that there is little people can do to reduce such problems. Global effects are the products of local actions. Macrosocial applications of sociocognitive principles via the electronic media illustrate how small collective efforts can have huge impacts on such urgent global problems as the soaring population growth.

Personality as Integrated Self System

Sociocognitive theories are commonly misconstrued as atomistic without an overreaching "personality." The umbrella term "personality" represents a complex of interacting attributes not a self-contained entity describable by a few pithy terms creating the illusion of a high-order structure. Personality is multifaceted, richly contextualized, and conditionally expressed in the diverse transactions of everyday life. The totality of an individual's cognitive, behavioral, and affective proclivities is not shrinkable to a few static descriptive categories.

People express their individuality and give structure, meaning and purpose to their lives by acting on their beliefs about themselves, their values, personal standards, aspirations and construals of the world around them. These multiform belief systems, self structures and selfreferent processes through which one's "personality" is manifested in its totality function in concert not isolatedly. It is through coordinative and integrative activity that the diverse sources of influence produce unity of experience and action. The self embodies all of the endowments, belief systems and distributed structures and functions through which personal agency is exercised rather than residing as a discrete entity in a particular place. In short, the self is the person not a homunculian subpart. "Personality" is the integrated self system within which the previously identified constituents operate in complex mutual interaction in the management of diverse and changing environmental circumstances.

The various constituents must be orchestrated in an integrated way because, whatever options are considered, the choices finally made and the actions taken at a given time require unity of agency. Given but a single body, one cannot perform incompatible acts simultaneously. People may, of course, exhibit contradictory behavior, but these are instances of the same being doing discordant things on different occasions not different selves doing their separate things. Personal identity refers to self-characterizations that tell what one is.

Social cognitive theory and research not only examine the individual properties of these key constituents but how they contribute to personal identity and functioning within the organized multifaceted system of determinants. The exercise of agency through the interrelated self structures and regulatory processes shapes the kind of life people live and what they consider themselves to be.

The personal identity they create for themselves derives, in large part, from how they live their life and reflect upon it. The continuity of personal identity resides more in psychological factors and the experiential continuity of the course of life followed than in physical constancy. An amnesic remains the same physically but has lost a sense of personal identity. Continuing selfidentity is preserved in memories that give temporal coherence to life, in continuance of belief and value commitments that link the present to the past and shape the course of future events, and in the connectedness of human relationships and one's life work over time.

Continuing self-identity is not solely a product of an intrapsychic autobiographical process that preserves a sense of personal continuity over time. Others perceive, socially label and treat one as the same person over the course of life. Personal identity is partially constructed from one's social identity as reflected in how one is treated by significant others. In keeping with the model of triadic reciprocal causation, a sense of selfhood is the product of a complex interplay of social and personal construal processes. Others, of course, have only a limited sample of a given person's social life and know even much less of that individual's experiential life. Consequently, the social identity conveyed by others is more heavily dependent on the sameness of physical characteristics, social roles, and habitual behaviors that are publicly observable than on personal uniqueness and experiential factors. Identity formation is an ongoing process not one characterized by fixedness in time. Moreover, the self view is multifaceted rather than monolithic. There are many aspects to the self. They are not equally salient, valued, or functional in different spheres of life or under different circumstances. In a dynamic, multifaceted model, continuity of personal identity requires neither high consistency among different aspects of self nor invariance across different social environments or domains of functioning. For given individuals, their personal identities are likely to be composed of unique amalgams of identities with national, social, political, ethnic, occupational, and familial aspects of life depending on their value commitments. Thus, for a particular individual, a strong occupational identity may coexist with a moderate ethnic identity and a weak political identity without any felt discordance because these aspects differ in the value placed on them.

Another individual, with dissimilar value commitments, may exhibit a quite different constellation of identities, combining a strong ethnic and political identity with a weak occupational identity. Similarly, a person's self view with parents may differ significantly from the self view in relationships with peers because these social worlds actualize different aspects of the self. In each case, however, it is one and the same person manifesting a multifaceted personal identity. It is the temporal stability of the patterned self view rather than high coherence of aspects that defines one's personal uniqueness and sense of continuity. Theories that construe personal identity as a fixed monolith are discordant with a vast body of evidence. With further experiences over time, people evolve and integrate some new aspects into their self-identity. This raises the issue of how they extract continuity from variability across time, activity domains, and social contexts. To the extent that they consider mainly core aspects or focus on different aspects of themselves as relevant in different life situations, they can change in particulars but preserve a sense of continuity in their view of themselves. However, if they undergo major life changes, they consider themselves to be different persons from whom they were in the past. Taken as a whole, the findings of diverse lines of research on the various personal properties subsumed under the spacious construct of "personality," attest to the explanatory, predictive and operative efficacy of theories that specify multiform personal structures operating conditionally through self-regulatory mechanisms within the contextual influences in which people construct and conduct their lives.

Impact of Evolutionary Factors

Social cognitive theory acknowledges the influential role of evolutionary factors in human adaptation and change, but rejects one-sided evolutionism in which social behavior is the product of evolved biology but social and technological innovations that create new environmental selection pressures for adaptiveness have no effect on biological evolution. In the bidirectional view of evolutionary processes, evolutionary pressures fostered changes in biological structures and upright posture conducive to the development and use of tools, which enabled an organism to manipulate, alter and construct new environmental conditions.

Environmental innovations of increasing complexity, in turn, created new selection pressures for the evolution of specialized biological systems for functional consciousness, thought, language and symbolic communication. All too often, the multicausality of human behavior is misleadingly framed in terms of partitioning behavioral variance into percent nature and percent nurture. This causal dualism is mistaken for several reasons. It disregards the interdependence of nature and nurture. Socially constructed nurture has a hand in shaping nature. It also fails to address fundamental issues concerning the operational nature of human nature.

Human evolution provides bodily structures and biological potentialities not behavioral dictates. Psychosocial influences operate through these biological resources in the construction and regulation of human behavior acting in the service of diverse purposes. Having evolved, the advanced biological capacities can be used to create diverse cultures-aggressive ones, pacific ones, egalitarian ones or autocratic ones. As Gould notes, biology sets constraints that vary in nature, degree and strength across different spheres of functioning, but in most domains of human functioning biology permits a broad range of cultural possibilities. He argues cogently that evidence favors a potentialist view over a determinist view. In this insightful analysis, the major explanatory battle is not between nature and nurture as commonly portrayed, but whether nature operates as a determinist or as a potentialist. He makes the further interesting point that biological determinism is often clothed in the language of interactionism, to make it more palatable. The bidirectional biology-culture coevolution is acknowledged but then the major causation of human behavior is ascribed to evolved biology. The cultural side of this two-way causation, in which genetic make-up is shaped by the adaptational pressures of socially constructed environments, receives little notice.

Biological determinism is also often clothed in the language of changeability: The malleability of evolved proclivities is acknowledged but determinative potency is then ascribed to them with caution against efforts to change existing sociostructural arrangements and practices allegedly ruled by evolved dispositions. Such efforts are regarded as not only doomed to failure but socially harmful because they go against the rule of nature. The conception of the operational nature of human nature affects the relative explanatory weight given to genetic mismatch and to the counterforce of entrenched vested interests for resistance to sociostructural changes. Biological determinists favor heavily the rule of nature, whereas biological potentialists see human nature as permitting a range of possibilities that gives greater saliency to the rule of distributed opportunities, privileges and power. Thus, a biological determinist view highlights inherent constraints and limitations. A biological potentialist view of human nature emphasizes multiform human possibilities. Theories that heavily attribute human social behavior to the rule of nature are disputed by the remarkable cultural diversity. Consider aggression, which is presumably genetically programmed as a biological universal and more so for males than for females. There are three types of cultural diversity that challenge the view that people are inherently aggressive.

— *Intercultural diversity:* There are fighting cultures that breed aggression by modeling it pervasively, attaching prestige to it, and according it functional value for gaining social status, material benefits and social control. There are pacific cultures in which interpersonal aggression is a rarity because it is devalued, rarely modeled and has no functional value. Is the genetic make-up of the Germans who perpetrated unprecedented barbarity really different from the genetic make-up of peaceable Swiss residing in the German canton of Switzerland? People possess the biological potentiality for aggression, but the answer to the differential aggressiveness in the latter case lies more in ideology than in biology.

— Variability concerns intracultural diversity.

— Variability involves rapid transformation of warring societies into peaceful ones.

The process of biological selection moves at a snails pace, whereas societies have been undergoing major changes in sexual mores, family structures, social and occupational roles and institutional practices. Ancestral origin and the determinants governing contemporary social practices are quite different matters. Because evolved potentialities can serve diverse purposes, ancestral origin dictates neither current function nor a singular sociostructural arrangement.

Social systems and practices are being changed by social means rather than by reliance on the slow protracted process of biological selection. Seen from the social cognitive perspective, human nature is characterized by a vast potentiality that can be fashioned by direct and vicarious experience into a variety of forms within biological limits. To say that a major distinguishing mark of humans is their endowed plasticity is not to say that they have no nature or that they come structureless.

The plasticity, which is intrinsic to the nature of humans, depends upon specialized neurophysiological structures and mechanisms that have evolved over time. These advanced neural systems are specialized for channeling attention, detecting the causal structure of the world around one, transforming that information into abstract form, integrating it and using it for adaptive purposes.

The evolved morphology and special purpose systems facilitate acquisitional processes. Social cognitive theory does not assume an equipotential mechanisms of learning. In addition to biological biases, some things are more easily learnable because the properties of the events can facilitate or impede acquisitional processes. The evolved informative processing systems provide the capacity for the very characteristics that are distinctly human-generative symbolization, forethought, evaluative self-regulation, reflective selfconsciousness, and symbolic communication.

Although neurophysiological systems have been shaped by evolutionary pressures, people are not just reactive products of selection pressures. They are producers of new selection pressures. Through agentic action, they devise ways of adapting flexibly to remarkably diverse environments, they circumvent environmental constraints, redesign and construct environments to their liking, create styles of behavior that enable them to realize desired outcomes and pass on the effective ones to others by social modeling and other experiential means. Indeed, growth of knowledge has greatly enhanced human power to control, transform and create environments of increasing complexity. We build physical technologies that drastically alter how we live daily lives; we create mechanical devices that compensate immensely for sensory and physical limitations; we develop medical and psychological methods that enable

2

Children and Gender Development

Gender development is the primary basis on which people get differentiated with pervasive effects on their daily lives. Gender differentiation takes on added importance because many of the attributes and roles selectively promoted in males and females tend to be differentially valued with those ascribed to males generally being regarded as more desirable, effectual and of higher status. Although some gender differences are biologically founded, most of the stereotypic attributes and roles linked to gender arise more from cultural design than from biological endowment.

Theories of Gender Development

Several theories are proposed to explain gender development. They differ on several important dimensions. One dimension concerns the relative emphasis placed on psychological, biological, and sociostructural determinants. Psychologically-oriented theories tend to emphasize intrapsychic processes governing gender development. In contrast, sociological theories focus on sociostructural determinants of gender-role development and functioning. According to biologically-oriented theories, gender differences arising from the differential biological roles played by males and females in reproduction underlie gender-role development and differentiation. A second dimension concerns the nature of the transmission models. Psychological theories typically emphasize the cognitive construction of gender conceptions and styles of behavior within the familial transmission model.

Behavioristic theories also have accorded prominence to parents in shaping and regulating gender-linked conduct. In theories favoring biological determinants, familial genes are posited as the transmission agent of gender differentiation across generations. Sociologically-oriented theories emphasize the social construction of gender roles mainly at the institutional level. Social cognitive theory of gender-role development and functioning integrates psychological and sociostructural determinants within a unified conceptual framework. In this perspective, gender conceptions and role behavior are the products of a broad network of social influences operating both familially and in the many societal systems encountered in everyday life. Thus, it favors a multifaceted social transmission model rather than mainly a familial transmission model. The third dimension concerns the temporal scope of the theoretical analyses. Most psychological theories treat gender development as primarily a phenomenon of early childhood rather than one that operates throughout the life course. However, rules of gender-role conduct vary to some degree across social contexts and at different periods in life. Moreover, sociocultural and technological changes necessitate revision of pre-existing conceptions of what constitutes appropriate gender conduct.

Gender role development and functioning are not confined to childhood but are negotiated throughout the life course. While most theories of gender development have been concerned with the early years of development, sociocognitive theory takes a life-course perspective. Therefore, in the following sections, the analysis of the sociocognitive determinants of gender orientations will span the entire age range. Nor is the theory restricted predominantly to cognitive or social factors. Rather cognitive, social, affective and motivational processes are all accorded prominence. Before presenting the sociocognitive perspective on gender development, the main psychological, biological and sociological perspectives on gender differentiation are briefly reviewed.

Psychoanalytic Theory

Psychoanalytic theory posited different processes to explain gender development in boys and girls. Initially, both boys and girls are believed to identify with their mothers. However, between 3 to 5 years of age this changes and children identify with the same-sex parent. Identification with the same-sex parent is presumed to resolve the conflict children experience as a result of erotic attachment to the opposite-sex parent and jealousy toward the same-sex parent. This attachment causes children much anxiety as they fear retaliation from the same-sex parent. The lack of a visible genitalia in girls fuels boys' castration anxieties. Girls face a more complex situation. They feel resentment over being deprived of a penis, inferior, and fear retaliation from the mother for their designs on their father. The conflicting relationship is resolved through identification with the same-sex parent. The process of identification is depicted as one in which children undertake wholesale adoption of the characteristics and qualities of the same-sex parent. Through this process of identification, children become sex-typed. Because identification with the same-sex parent is stronger for boys than girls, boys are expected to be more strongly sex-typed. Although psychoanalytic theory has had a pervasive early influence in developmental psychology, there is little empirical evidence to support it.

A clear relationship between identification with the same-sex parent and gender-role adoption has never been empirically verified. Children are more likely to model their behavior after nurturant models or socially powerful ones than after threatening models with whom they have a rivalrous relationship. Lack of empirical support for classic psychoanalytic theory has led to a variety of reformulations of it. Gender identification begins in infancy rather than during the later phallic stage as proposed by Freud. Both male and female infants initially identify with their mother. However, because the mother is of the same sex as her daughter, identification is expected to be stronger between mothers and their daughters than between mothers and their sons. During the course of development, girls continue to identify with their mothers and they also psychologically merge with her. As a consequence, the daughter's self-concept is characterized by mutuality and a sense of relatedness that orients her towards interpersonal relationships. This interpersonal orientation is the main reason why women engage in mothering. They seek to reestablish a sense of interpersonal connectedness reminiscent of their relationship with their mother but absent in their adult relationships with men. This pattern of development contrasts with that of boys who increasingly separate themselves from their mothers and define themselves in terms of difference from females. They begin to denigrate femininity in an attempt to establish their own separateness and individuation.

The empirical findings, however, are no more supportive of Chodorow's theory than of classic psychoanalytic theory. There is no evidence that the attachment bond is any stronger between mothers and daughters than mothers and sons. Nor is there any evidence that women's relational needs and sense of well-being are fulfilled only by being mothers. Women whose sole role is one of mother and wife have higher rates of mental dysfunction than childless married and single women and working mothers. Finally, this theory is at odds with women's striving for greater independence and equality between the sexes.

Cognitive Developmental Theory

According to cognitive developmental theory, gender identity is postulated as the basic organizer and regulator of children's gender learning. Children develop the stereotypic conceptions of gender from what they see and hear around them. Once they achieve gender constancy—the belief that their own gender is fixed and irreversible—they positively value their gender identity and seek to behave only in ways that are congruent with that conception. Cognitive consistency is gratifying, so individuals attempt to behave in ways that are consistent with their self-conception. Much of children's conduct is designed to confirm their gender identity. Once children establish knowledge of their own gender, the reciprocal interplay between one's behavior (acting like a girl) and thoughts (I am a girl) leads to a stable gender identity, or in cognitive-developmental theory terms, the child achieves gender constancy. Kohlberg defined gender constancy as the realization that one's sex is a permanent attribute tied to underlying biological properties and does not depend on superficial characteristics such as hair length, style of clothing, or choice of play activities.

Development of gender constancy is not an all or none phenomenon. Three discrete levels of gender understanding comprise gender constancy. From least to most mature forms of gender understanding, these are designated as the gender identity, stability, and consistency components of gender constancy. "Gender identity" requires the simple ability to label oneself as a boy or girl and others as a boy, girl, man, or woman. "Gender stability" is the recognition that gender remains constant over time-that is, one's sex is the same now as it was when one was a baby and will remain the same in adulthood. The final component of gender constancy, "gender consistency", is mastered at about age six or seven years. The child now possesses the added knowledge that gender is invariant despite changes in appearance, dress or activity. Children are not expected to adopt gender-typed behaviors consistently until after they regard themselves unalterably as a boy or a girl, which usually is not achieved until about six years of age. Although Kohlberg's theory attracted much attention over the decades, its main tenets have not fared well empirically. Studies generally have failed to corroborate the link between children's attainment of gender constancy and their gender-linked conduct. Long before children have attained gender constancy, they prefer to play with toys traditionally associated with their gender, to model their behavior after same-sex models, and to reward peers for gender—appropriate behavior.

Moreover, growing awareness of gender constancy does not increase children's preferences for same-gender roles and activities. The findings of other lines of research similarly fail to support the major tenets of this theory. Although stable gender constancy is not attained until about six years of age, 2-year olds perform remarkably well in sorting pictures of feminine and masculine toys, articles of clothing, tools and appliances in terms of their typical gender relatedness.

Children's ability to classify their own and others' sex and some knowledge of gender-role stereotypes is all that is necessary for much early gender typing to occur. These categorization skills are evident in most three- and four-year olds. Clearly, gender constancy is not a prerequisite for gender development. Factors other than gender constancy govern children's gender-linked conduct. In response to the negative findings, the gender constancy measure was modified to demonstrate that the assessment procedure rather than the theory is at fault for the lack of linkage of gender constancy to gender conduct.

The modifications included altering the inquiry format, the use of more realistic stimuli, and less reliance on verbal responses. Although some of these modifications showed that children understand gender constancy earlier than most children under 4 years do not fully understand the concept of constancy regardless of the form of its assessment.

More importantly, there is no relationship between children's understanding of gender constancy and their preference for gender-linked activities, preference for same-gender peers, or emulation of same-gender models, regardless of how gender constancy is assessed.

Gender Schema Theory

Several gender schema theories have been proposed to explain gender development and differentiation. The social psychological approaches advanced by Bem and Markus and her associates have centered mainly on individual differences in gender schematic processing of information. The theory has many similarities to cognitive-developmental theory, but departs from it in several ways. Rather than requiring the attainment of gender constancy for development of gender orientations, only the mastery of gender identity, the ability of children to label themselves and others as males or females, is considered necessary for gender schema development to begin. Once formed, it is posited that the schema expands to include knowledge of activities and interests, personality and social attributes, and scripts about gender-linked activities. The schema is presumably formed from interactions with the environment, but the process by which gender features that constitute the knowledge structure of the schema are abstracted remain unspecified.

Once the schema is developed, children are expected to behave in ways consistent with traditional gender roles. The motivating force guiding children's gender-linked conduct, as in cognitive developmental theory, relies on gender-label matching in which children want to be like others of their own sex. Results of empirical tests call into question the determinative role of gender schema. The evidence linking gender labeling to activity and peer preferences is mixed at best. A few studies have found a link, others report conflicting results across different measures of gender-linked conduct, and still others have failed to find any link at all. Even in the studies that report a relationship, it remains to be determined whether gender labeling and gender-linked preferences are causally linked or are merely coeffects of social influences and cognitive abilities. Parents who react evaluatively to gender-linked conduct have children who are early gender labelers. Hence, gender labeling and preference may both be products of parental influence.

Knowledge of gender stereotypes, which are generalized preconceptions about the attributes of males and females, is similarly unrelated to gender-linked conduct. Children's preferences for gendered activities emerge before they know the gender linkage of such activities. A gender schema represents a more generic knowledge structure about maleness and femaleness. Gender schema theory would predict that the more elaborated the gender knowledge children possess, the more strongly they should show gender-linked preferences. However, this hypothesized relationship receives no empirical support. Adults, may be fully aware of gender stereotypes but this does not produce incremental prediction of gender-linked conduct as such knowledge increases. These various results fail to confirm gender knowledge as the determinant of gender-linked conduct.

Gender schema theory has provided a useful framework for examining the cognitive processing of gender information once gender schemas are developed.

In particular, it has shed light on how genderschematic processing affects attention, organization, and memory of gender-related information. Other models of gender schema that focus on adults have similarly demonstrated gender biases in information processing. The more salient or available the schema, the more individuals are expected to attend to, encode, represent, and retrieve information relevant to gender. However, gender-schematic processing is unrelated to either children's or adult's gender conduct or the findings are inconsistent across different measures of gender schematization. A gender schema is not a monolithic entity. Children do not categorize themselves as "I am girl" or "I am a boy" and act in accordance with that schema invariantly across situations and activity domains. Rather they vary in their gender conduct depending on a variety of circumstances. Variability is present at the adult level as well. A woman may be a hard-driving manager in the workplace but a traditionalist in the functions performed in the home.

The problems with a multiple-self theory have been addressed elsewhere and will be mentioned only briefly here. It requires a regress to a superordinate self who has to manage the inharmonious subselves. There is really only one self that can do diverse things, including discordant ones on different occasions and under different circumstances. The selective engagement and disengagement of self-regulatory mechanisms by the same being predict variation in conduct, including contradictory styles of behavior. A further limitation of gender schema theory is that it cannot explain the asymmetry in findings between boys and girls. Boys and girls differ in the extent to which they prefer same-gender activities, emulate same-gender models and play with same-gender peers, yet most studies find no differences in girls' and boys' gender stereotypic knowledge. Both cognitive-developmental theory and gender schema theory have focused on gender conceptions, but neither devotes much attention to the mechanisms by which gender-linked conceptions are acquired and translated to gender-linked conduct. Nor do they specify the motivational mechanism for acting in accordance with a conception. Knowing a stereotype does not necessarily mean that one strives to behave in accordance with it. For example, self-conception as an elderly person does not enhance valuation and eager adoption of the negative stereotypic behavior of old age. Evidence that gender conception is insufficient to explain variations in gender-linked conduct should not be misconstrued as negation of cognitive determinants. As will be explained in subsequent sections, social cognitive theory posits a variety of motivational and self-regulatory mechanisms rooted in cognitive activity that regulate gender development and functioning. These include, among other things, cognitions concerning personal efficacy, evaluative standards, aspirations, outcome expectations rooted in a value system, and perception of sociostructural opportunities and constraints.

Biological Theories

Biologically-oriented theories have also been proposed to explain gender development and differentiation. Evolutionary psychology is one such theory that views gender differentiation as ancestrally programmed. The ancestral origin of differences in gender roles is analyzed in terms of mate preferences, reproductive strategies, parental investment in offspring, and the aggressive nature of males. Viewed from this perspective, contemporary gender differences originated from successful ancestral adaptation to the different reproductive demands faced by men and women. Men contributed less to their offsprings' chances of survival so they sought multiple partners and were less choosy with whom to mate. In addition, uncertainty of paternity raised the risk of investing resources in children who were not their own. In contrast, women have to carry the fetus and care for their offspring years after their birth. Women adapted to their greater imposed role in reproduction and parenting by preferring fewer sexual partners and favoring those who would be good long-term providers of the basic necessities of life for themselves and their offspring. Men, in contrast, attempted to maximize the likelihood of paternity by reproducing with numerous young and physically attractive females, suggestive of high fertility. Because of their size and strength advantage, males resolved problems arising from conflicting reproductive interests by exercising aggressive dominance over females. Coercive force enables males to control female's sexuality and to mate with many females. As a legacy of this evolutionary history, women have come to invest more heavily than men in parenting roles. Males, in turn, evolved into aggressors, social dominators and prolific maters because such behavior increased their success in propagating their genes.

According to evolutionary psychology, many current gender differences, such as the number of sexual partners preferred, criteria for selecting sexual partners, aggression, jealousy and the roles they fulfill originated from the ancestral sex differentiated reproductive strategies. For example, the findings that men prefer women who are young and physically attractive and women prefer men who are financially well resourced as mates are considered supportive of biological selection. Not all evolutionary theorists speak with one voice, however. Psychological evolutionists often take a more extreme deterministic stance regarding the rule of nature than do many biological evolutionists. Psychological evolutionists are also quick to invoke evolved behavioral traits as cultural universals, whereas biological evolutionists emphasize functional relations between organism and situated environment that underscores the diversifying selection influence of variant ecological contexts. It should also be noted that evolutionary psychology grounds gender differences in ancestral mating strategies, but it does not address at all the developmental changes that occur in gender conceptions and gendered conduct. Nor does it specify the determinants and mechanisms governing developmental changes across the life course.

Natural selection shapes for proximate utility not future purpose. Bodily structures and biological potentialities are shaped by the aimless forces of natural selection acting on random mutations or new gene recombinations. Depiction of ancestral males as seeking to maximize paternity and of ancestral females as looking for good providers suggest that they are acting on deliberate or tacit purpose. Strategies subserve goals. Such appending of purpose to mating patterns and calling them "strategies," which are designed to bring about some goal, sounds more like a teleological explanation than a Darwinian functional explanation. Disclaimers that the strategies are not always in awareness still leaves them undertaken for some particular end. Moreover, it is conceptually and methodologically problematic to use mindful self-ratings as the indicants of mating preferences to which the individuals supposedly have no conscious access. The claim that evolutionary psychology provides the solution to the origin of gender differences in social behavior simply raises the regress problem. For example, evolutionary explanations that attribute mating practices to "strategies" rather than to the work of blind selection forces beg the question of why males should seek to maximize paternity. Evolutionary psychology is proposed as a superior alternative to more socially oriented explanations of gender differentiation. However, this view, which attributes overriding power to biology, is not without serious problems. It is mainly a descriptive and post hoc explanatory device that lacks the scientific rigor required of evolutionary analyses. What were the environmental pressures operating during the ancestral era when the differential reproductive strategies were allegedly developed? Neither molecular evidence from fossilized human remains nor detailed archaeological artifacts are provided to support the evolutionary storytelling about ancestral environmental selection pressures and the accompanying changes in genetic make-up.

The genetic variation on which selection forces could have operated in the past of course remains unknown, but is there any evidence of genetic differences between present-day philanderers and monogamists? What empirical evidence is there that males prefer young fertile-looking females and females prefer richly-resourced males because of different genes? Psychological evolutionism does not provide the mechanisms responsible for social patterns of behavior, nor does it specify the nature of the interactional relationship between genetic and environmental influences for disentangling their impact. Contrary to claims, predictions from psychological evolutionism are not consistently supported in comparative tests of evolutionary and sociostructural theories or by the attributes males and females prefer in their mates. Some theorists, even question the evolutionary validity of some of the predictions made from evolutionary biology by psychological evolutionists.

Others challenge universalized predictions that are evolutionally relevant but portray organisms as disembodied from variant ecological conditions under which they live that present quite different selection pressures. Variations in ecological selective forces promote different adaptational patterns of behavior. To add to the cultural diversity, belief systems about how reproduction works perpetuate distinctive mating patterns. For example, in societies where people believe it requires cumulative insemination by multiple partners to produce a baby, women have sexual intercourse with different men without attendant sexual jealousy. According to evolutionary psychology, the biological basis of gender differentiation has changed little since the ancestral era. Since prehistoric times there have been massive cultural and technological innovations that have drastically altered how people live their lives. A theory positing genetic fixedness over this evolutionary period has major explanatory problems given that contemporary women are markedly different in preferences, attributes and social and occupational roles from the ancestral ones in the hunter-gatherer era. Indeed, for the most part, present day lifestyle patterns and reproduction practices run counter to the speculative scenarios of psychological evolutionism. Birthrates have declined markedly. Males are not fathering numerous offspring to ensure continuance of copies of their genes. Quite the contrary. Contraceptive devices have disjoined sex from procreation and provided control over the number and timing of childbearing.

Consequently, males are putting their inherited copulatory mechanism to frequent use but relying on contraceptive means to prevent paternity! They are seeking nonreproductive sexual gratification and other sources of satisfactions not reproductive success, which is the prime driving force for heterosexual and intermale relations in psychological evolutionism. In short, through contraceptive ingenuity, humans have outwitted and taken control over their evolved reproductive system. Given the prevalence of contraceptive sexuality, the claim that male preference for multiple physically attractive females is evolutionarily driven to maximize paternity sounds more like social justification for male philandering. The heavy biologizing of gender roles also seems divorced from the changing roles of females in contemporary society. Most are combining occupational pursuits with homemaking rather than being confined to childbearing domesticity. The substantial modification in reproduction practices and attendant lifestyle changes were ushered in by technological innovations in contraception not by the slow biological selection.

Aggressive skill may have had reproductive advantage in ancient times when males could lay claim to females at will, but cultural evolution of social norms and sanctions has essentially stripped it of reproductive benefit. Some males rule females by physical force, but most do not. Physical and sexual aggressors are more likely to populate prisons than the gene pool. Reproduction rates are governed mainly by sociocultural norms, socioeconomic status, religious beliefs and adoption of contraceptive methods rather than by aggressive proclivities and skill in intermale aggression. The methods and data used by psychological evolutionists to link ancestral gender differentiation to current gendered preferences, attributes and roles have also come under fire. The research relies mainly on survey studies using rating scales without the type of detailed analysis of genetic make-up and genetic transmission mechanisms conducted in the evolutionary tradition. Surprisingly, mating behavior is rarely measured. For example, evidence for gender differences in the types of partners selected is based mainly on self-reported preferences rather than on actual choices.

Evolutionary processes are governed by what people do not by what they say. If physically attractive females are the objects of sexual pursuit, what evidence is there that the attractive ones are selectively impregnated at higher rates than those regarded as less attractive according to the prevailing cultural standards? Preference ratings cannot substitute for impregnation rates. Contrary to the view that parenting is the prime investment of women, men in long-term partnerships invest extensively in their offspring and are quite selective in their choice of mates. The conversion of typicality ratings into proclivitive universalities is another major problem. Small gender differences in the statistical average of self-reported preferences for a spread of ratings that overlap markedly across the genders get invoked as universal biological proclivities ascribed to males and females as though they all behaved alike as dichotomously classified. The substantial diversity within gender groups, which an adequate theory must explain, is simply ignored. Survey reports in which males say that, on average, they would like about 18 sexual partners, whereas women would settle for about 4 or 5 mates, are cited as corroborating evolutionary psychological theory. There is a big difference between verbalized preference and action. The more relevant data regarding male mating are what males do rather than what they say, and the variation in sexual practices among men.

The explanatory challenge for psychological evolutionism is why most males mate monogamously, and relatively few roam around impregnating young fertile females to populate the gene pool for subsequent generations. If prolific uncommitted sexuality is a male biological imperative, it must be an infirm one that can be easily overridden by psychosocial forces. Why married women would get sexually involved with multiple men, and thereby risk jealous assaults and loss of resources provided by the long-term mate is also problematic for psychological evolutionism. An explanation in terms of seeking socioemotional satisfaction and nonreproductive sexual pleasure is more plausible than ad hoc explanations that they are seeking better genes, supplemental resources or richer providers. One can, of course, construct evolutionary scenarios of evolved genetic dispositions for males behaving as uncommitted sexual free lancers but then as committed monogamists, and homebody females as straying into infidelity. But such temporally flexible explanations, in which biological dispositions suddenly reverse direction from promoting philandering to upholding monogamy, are more like ad hoc theorizing (i.e., whatever gendered patterns appear currently must be products of natural selection) than as derivations from an integrated core theory.

Evolutionary psychology fails to specify a mechanism governing the posited dispositional reversal, what triggers it, and when the reversal should occur. Not all males necessarily go through a philandering phase before settling down to a monogamous life. This casts serious doubt on the inherentness of the posited temporal sequencing of reproductive "strategies." How does the genetically-driven disposition know when a heterosexual relationship is a short-term affair or the beginning of what will become an enduring monogamous relationship? Many of the human characteristics that are sexually arousing-corpulence or skinniness; upright breasts or long pendulous ones; shiny white teeth or black pointed ones; distorted ears, noses or lips; light skin color or dark-not only vary markedly across societies, but bear no relevance to "good genes" or reproductive fertility and value. Human sexual arousal is driven more by the mind through cultural construction of attractiveness than by physical universals. As indicated in the preceding comments, there is often selective inattention to discordant aspects of the very type of evidence marshaled in support of psychological evolutionism. Human aggression provides a further example. In fact, only a minute fraction of humans ever commit a homicide. Given the stiff competitiveness for desirable mates, the explanatory challenge for psychological evolutionism is why an intermale assaultive disposition that is considered so central in mate access and control is so rarely manifested. Nor can evolutionary factors explain large fluctuations in homicide rates over short periods, which are largely tied to level of drug activities rather than to reproduction battles.

Of the small number of people who happen to kill, they do so for all sorts of reasons, the least of which may be a drive to maximize paternity. With regard to intergender violence, sexual assaults against women are prevalent in societies where male supremacy reigns, aggressive sexuality is valued as a sign of manliness and women are treated as property. In contrast, sexual assaults are rare in societies that repudiate interpersonal aggression, endorse sexual equality and treat women respectfully. The extensive cross-cultural and intracultural variability in male-female power relations and physical and sexual violence toward women, disputes the view that using physical force against women is the rule of nature. Ancestral origin and the determinants governing contemporary social practices are quite different matters. Because evolved potentialities can serve diverse purposes, ancestral origin dictates neither current function nor singular sociostructural arrangements. Did ancestral mating pressures really create a biological imperative to deny women voting rights until 1926 in the United States, disallow them property rights; give men custody of children even though child caretaking is supposedly not men's inherent nature; curtail women's educational opportunities; bar them from entry into prestigious universities such as Yale until 1969; deny them equal pay for comparable work; impede their efforts to secure occupational advancements at upper organizational ranks; and refuse them membership in clubs where social networking and business transactions spawn occupational successes? Evidence to be presented later suggests that the inequitable gender differentiation just described reflects, in large part, the constraints of custom and gender power and privilege imbalances in how the societal subsystems that preside over gender development are structured and operate.

Other analyses of gender differences from a biological perspective have centered on hormonal influences and estimates of heritability. Hormones affect the organization of the neural substrates of the brain, including lateralization of brain function. It has been reported that females show less lateral brain specialization than do males, but the differences are small and some studies find no such difference. Difference in degree of brain lateralization is assumed to produce gender differences in cognitive processing. Although girls generally do better on verbal tasks, and boys do better on some types of mathematical tasks, the differences are small. Moreover, the gender differences have been diminishing over the past decade, which is much too short a time to be genetically determined. However, there are clear and reliable differences in spatial skills favoring males. But this difference has also been diminishing in recent years, most likely as a function of social changes. Although hormones may play a part in spatial ability, the evidence suggests that environmental factors play a central role in the observed differences. Compared to girls, boys grow up in more spatially complex environments, receive more encouragement for outdoor play, and engage extensively in activities that foster the development of spatial skills. In accord with a social source, gender differences in spatial ability are not found in cultures where women are granted greater freedom of action. The search for a hormonal basis for gender differences in social behavior has produced highly conflicting results. Despite considerable research, the influence of hormones on behavioral development and cognitive functioning remains unclear. Drawing on atypical populations in which the developing fetus is exposed to high levels of prenatal male or female hormones, the findings show that girls increase engagement in traditionally male-and female-related activities, respectively.

The causal link between hormones and behavior, however, has not been established. Because these children often look different from other children of their own sex and parents are very much aware of their atypical condition, hormonal influences cannot be disentangled from social ones. In addition, the lack of relationship between prenatal hormones and gender-linked behavior for boys raises further questions about whether hormonal factors could be the basis for gender-differentiated conduct. Because of the empirical inconclusiveness and methodological problems associated with research on atypical populations, researchers have turned to studying conduct as a function of variations in hormonal levels where no abnormality exists prenatally. However, these findings not only fail to support those from atypical populations, but contradict them. For example, girls with naturally high levels of male hormones prenatally show low spatial ability in childhood, but girls with elevated male hormones prenatally occurring either artificially or from a genetic defect show high spatial ability. However, boys' spatial ability is unaffected by their prenatal hormonal levels. To add to the conflicting findings, male hormones in late adolescence and adulthood are weakly related to aggressive and antisocial conduct for males but not for females, whereas in childhood and early adolescence male hormones predict aggression for girls but not for boys. If the conditions governing this variability are identified, it would still remain to be determined whether hormonal levels are the cause or the effect of aggressive conduct or whether they operate only indirectly by lowering tolerance of frustration.

Researchers working within the framework of behavioral genetics examine gender differences in terms of the relative contribution of environmental and genetic factors to variation in given attributes. Identical and fraternal twins reared apart in different environments are tested for differences on a variety of cognitive abilities and personality characteristics. Based on the results of such studies, it is concluded that genetic factors make low to moderate contribution to personality attributes. Most of the remaining variance is ascribed to nonshared environments unique to individual family members with little of it left to shared environments common to all members of the family. Although most of this research has focused on individual differences in general, several studies of children's gender-linked personality characteristics, namely masculinity and femininity, also report heritability estimates ranging from small to moderate. The findings reveal a substantial contribution of nonshared environmental influences to these gendered personality characteristics. The above results have led to downgrading parental influences on children's development and upgrading the impact of peers as a nonshared environment. However, this conclusion relies for its plausibility on a disputable environmental dualism and highly questionable assumptions on how social subsystems function. As will be shown later, parental and peer subsystems operate interdependently not as disjoined entities. Parents play an active role in structuring peer associations, fostering peer ties that are to their liking and discouraging those they disfavor.

Children who adopt parental values and standards choose friends on the basis of parental values. Consequently, the peer group serves to reinforce and uphold parental values. In discordant families, children may pick peer associates who bring them into conflict with their parents. Even in the latter case, parents also exert influence on peer selection, albeit through a rebuffing rather than adoptive process. Parents are also linked interdependently to the peer group through their children's communication about their activities with peers outside the home. Parents, in turn, offer social support and guidance on how to manage predicaments that arise in peer relations. Given the complex interplay of personal, familial, peer and other social influences, dichotomous partitioning of social environments into segregated shared and nonshared entities distorts rather than clarifies causal processes. It should also be noted that the estimates of the environment are almost always based on cursory self-reports rather than on actual observation of familial and extrafamilial interactions and social practices and the degree of bidirectionality of influence. Studies of the heritability of personality attributes rely almost exclusively on questionnaires that construe personality as global, decontextualized entities. In fact, personal proclivities are multifaceted, characterized by domain specificity and manifested contextually and conditionally. These global subdivisions of collections of ecologically-stripped behavior represent neither the nature nor structure of personal determinants, and say nothing about the self-regulatory mechanisms governing their conditional expression. The heritability of multifaceted dispositions that better capture the dynamic nature of personality remains to be determined.

Some attributes, such as height, are more heritable than others, such as aesthetic preferences. High heritability does not mean unmodifiability by environmental means. For example, although height is highly heritable, it can vary substantially as a function of quality of nutrition. Dull rats placed in an enriched environment performed as well as the bright ones reared normally, and bright rats placed in an impoverished environment performed as poorly as dull rats reared normally. Clearly, heritability does not ordain destiny.

The partitioning of behavioral variance into percent biology and percent environment flies in the face of their interdependence. Heritability refers to degree of genetic contribution to group variance not to individual causation. To explain individual behavior, which is typically the product of multicausality, one must specify how the relevant constellation of determinants operate in concert within the causal structure rather than try to compute the percent of the behavior due to nature and the percent due to nurture.

Sociological Theories

In sociological theories, gender is a social construction rather than a biological given. The sources of gender differentiation lie more in social and institutional practices than in fixed properties of the individual. Drawing on diverse bodies of research, documents masterfully the social construction and perpetuation of stereotypic gender differentiation. Gender stereotypes shape the perception, evaluation and treatment of males and females in selectively gendered ways that beget the very patterns of behavior that confirm the initial stereotypes. Many gender differences in social behavior are viewed as products of division of labor between the sexes that get replicated through sociostructural practices governed by disparate gender status and power. Many sociologists reject the dichotomous view of gender, in that the similarities between men and women in how they think and behave far exceed the differences between them. With social changes in opportunity structures and constraining institutional arrangements, gender differences have declined over time. Gender is not a unitary monolith.

The homogeneous gender typing disregards the vast differences among women and the similarly vast differences among men depending on their socioeconomic class, education, ethnicity, and occupation.

The practice of lumping all men and women into dichotomous gender categories, with men preordained for agentic functions and women for expressive and communion functions similarly comes in for heavy criticism. The exaggeration of the nature and extent of gender differences, the theorists argue, promotes the social ordering of gender relations and serves to justify gender inequality, occupational stratification and segregation, and the situating of women in positions of predominately lower status. Viewed from this sociological perspective, the pattern of opportunity structures and formal and informal constraints shape gendered styles of behavior and channel men and women into different life paths. The coupling of gender roles to biological sex status legitimates social arrangements as accommodations to differences attributed to inherent nature. Not all people of the same socioeconomic status, and who live under the same opportunity structures, social controls, familial, educational and community resources and normative climate, behave in the same way. The challenge is to explain adaptational diversity within sociostructural commonalty. As will be shown later, social cognitive theory adopts an integrated perspective in which sociostructural influences operate through self-system mechanisms to produce behavioral effects. However, the self system is not merely a conduit for external influences. People are producers as well as products of social systems. Social structures are created by human activity. The structural practices, in turn, impose constraints and provide resources and opportunity structures for personal development and functioning.

Modeling Influences

In addition to promoting differential styles of behavior, modeling influences can alter incentive motivation. Seeing others achieve valued outcomes by their efforts can instill motivating outcome expectancies in observers that they can secure similar benefits for comparable performances. Modeled performance outcomes thus create incentives and disincentives for action. By the same token, seeing others punished for engaging in certain activities can instill negative outcome expectations that serve as disincentives. These motivational effects rest on observers' judgments that they have the efficacy to produce the modeled performances and that comparable behavior will bring them similar outcomes. People are easily aroused by the emotional expressions of others. What gives significance to vicarious emotional influence is that observers can acquire lasting attitudes, and emotional and behavioral proclivities toward persons and activities that have been associated with modeled emotional experiences. They learn to fear things that frightened the models, to dislike what repulsed them, and to like what gratified them. Fears and behavioral restraints are reduced by modeling influences that convey information about coping strategies for exercising control over threats. The stronger the instilled sense of coping efficacy, the bolder the behavior. Values can similarly be developed and altered vicariously by repeated exposure to modeled preferences.

The actions of models can also serve as social prompts for previously learned behavior. The influence of models in activating, channeling, and supporting social behavior is abundantly documented in both laboratory and field studies. Thus, the types of models that prevail in a given social milieu partly determine which personal qualities, from among many alternatives, are selectively expressed. Most theories of gender development assign a major role to modeling in gender-role learning. They point to findings that, in laboratory situations, children do not consistently pattern their behavior after same-gender models. In everyday life, of course, children observe multiple exemplars in both their immediate environment and media representations of gender roles. The power of modeling is enhanced by typicality and similarity in role behavior within sex status. Indeed, in a set of studies varying the degree of modeled consensus the propensity of children to pattern their behavior after same-gender models increases as the percentage of same-gender models displaying the same conduct increases.

According to cognitive developmental theory, it is only after children have achieved gender constancy that they prefer to emulate models of the same gender. Gender constancy is viewed as an antecedent of modeling, rather than as a product of it. In social cognitive theory, repeated modeling of gender-typed behavior in the home, in schools, in workplaces, and in televised portrayals serves as a major conveyer of gender-role information. Through modeling and the structuring of social activities, children learn the prototypic behaviors associated with each of the sexes. In this view, gender constancy is the product rather than an antecedent of the emulation of same-sex models. When children observe models of their gender collectively exhibit stylistic behaviors that diverge from those displayed by other-gender models, children pattern their behavior more after same-gender than other-gender models. This preference for same-gender models occurs irrespective of children's level of gender constancy. After a more abstract conception of gender coupled with conditional outcome dependencies is formed, gender conceptions and gender-typed learning operate as bidirectional influences.

Social modeling operates at the collective level as well as individually. Modeling is a major social mechanisms through which behavioral patterns, social roles and sociostructural arrangements get replicated across generations. But modeling contributes to cultural evolution as well as to cultural transfer. When exposed to models who differ in their styles of thinking and behavior, observers rarely pattern their behavior exclusively after a single source, nor do they adopt all the attributes even of preferred models. Rather, observers typically combine various aspects of different models into new amalgams that differ from the individual sources. Because observers vary in what they adopt from the social diversity they observe, different observers create new blends of characteristics. Within their conceptual framework, multiple modeling influences, environmental conditions, and personal experiences operate interactively to change the distribution of cultural behavioral variants over time and to foster convergence toward variants that are especially efficacious in particular milieus. The different ways in which social learning influences favor some behavioral variants over others receive detailed consideration in the social cognitive theory of social diffusion of innovations. Moreover, symbolic modeling is an influential vehicle of rapid social change in contrast to the slower pace of incremental change. Challengers of inequitable social practices are enabled and motivated by the modeled successes of others who, under subordinating conditions, altered institutional practices by concerted collective action that changed their lives for the better.

Gender Roles and Conduct

People differ in how they respond to the same gender-linked conduct displayed by children. They can develop and refine gendered orientations by observing the positive and negative consequences accompanying different patterns of behavior. Moreover, some people are more concerned and reactive to gender-linked conduct. Fathers, for example, react more negatively than mothers to their sons' feminine toy play. The wider the array of people and social systems that children are exposed to and interact with, the more diverse the array of outcomes they experience for various types of gender-linked conduct. The same behavior can meet with different reactions from different people and in different contexts within the child's social milieu. Children extract, weigh and integrate this diverse outcome information in constructing guides for conduct.

Gender roles and conduct can be affected by direct tutoring as well as through modeling and social evaluative reactions. In this mode of influence gender conceptions are drawn from the tutelage of persons in one's social environment. As in other forms of influence, direct tuition is most effective when it is based on shared values and receives widespread social support. Models, of course, do not often practice what they preach. The impact of tuition is weakened when what is being taught is contradicted by what is modeled. Discordances between the style of behavior modeled by adults and peers adds further to the complexity of modeling processes. Children vary in the relative weight they give to the divergent sources of influence. As is evident from the preceding analysis, people do not passively absorb gender role conceptions from whatever influences happen to impinge upon them. Rather they construct generic conceptions from the diversity of styles of conduct that are modeled, evaluatively prescribed and taught by different individuals or by even the same person for different activities in different contexts. The development of gender role conceptions is a construction rather than simply a wholesale incorporation of what is socially transmitted.

The discussion thus far has centered on the acquisition of gender conceptions and competencies. This is only part of the theoretical framework. Social cognitive theory also addresses the factors that regulate gender-linked conduct and how their relative influence changes developmentally. These factors include self-regulatory mechanisms rooted in social sanctions and self sanctions. In addition, self-efficacy beliefs play a pivotal role in both the acquisition and regulation of gendered roles and styles of conduct.

Children have to gain predictive knowledge about the likely social outcomes of gender-linked conduct in different settings, toward different individuals and for different pursuits. The three basic modes of influence reviewed above similarly promote learning about the incentive structures of the social environment. Children acquire predictive outcome knowledge from observing the outcomes experienced by others, from the outcomes they experience first hand, and what they are told about the likely consequences of behaving in different ways for their sex. In the gender domain, most gender-linked outcomes are socially prescribed rather than intrinsic to the action.

They include socially based consequences such as approval, praise and reward for activities traditionally linked to the same gender, and disapproval or even punishment for those linked to the other gender. It is not naturally foreordained that the same behavior enacted by females should produce different outcomes than when enacted by males. In sociocognitive theory, evaluative social outcomes influence behavior mainly through their informational and motivational functions.

— Outcomes convey information about the social norms and the system of sanctions governing gender-linked behavior.

— Anticipated outcomes serve is as incentives and disincentives for action. Forethought converts foreseeable outcomes into current motivators of behavior. People pursue courses of action they believe will bring valued outcomes and refrain from those they believe will give rise to aversive outcomes.

The sociocognitive conception of incentive motivation, which combines the informational and motivational functions of social sanctions, differs from gender schema theory, which concerns only information about gender-linked stereotypes and gender identity. Simply knowing the stereotypes, which increase with age, do not necessarily motivate children to act in accord with them. Indeed, a meta-analytic study showed that as children become increasingly knowledgeable about gender-role stereotypes, they believe less strongly, especially girls, that those stereotypes should exist. Therefore, a comprehensive theory of gender development must consider not only knowledge about what is considered acceptable for the two sexes, but the motivation to act on that knowledge.

Social cognitive theory posits that, in the course of development, the regulation of behavior shifts from predominately external sanctions and mandates to gradual substitution of self sanctions and self direction grounded in personal standards. After self-regulatory functions are developed, children guide their conduct by sanctions they apply to themselves. They do things that give them self-satisfaction and a sense of self-worth. They refrain from behaving in ways that violate their standards to avoid self-censure. The standards provide the guidance; the anticipatory self-sanctions the motivators. Self-sanctions thus keep conduct in line with personal standards. Self-regulation operates through a set of psychological subfunctions that must be developed and mobilized for self-directed influence. These include self-monitoring of gender-linked conduct, judgment of conduct in relation to personal standards, and environmental circumstances, and self-reactive influence.

To exercise self-influence, people have to monitor their behavior and the situational circumstances in which they find themselves enmeshed. As children become aware of the social significance attached to gender, they increasingly attend to this aspect of their behavior. In mixed-sex groups children are more likely to monitor behavior according to its gender linkage. Compared to girls, boys monitor their behavior on the gender dimension more closely because, as already noted, they are more likely to be reproached for conduct that deviates from their gender. Moreover, boys have a strong incentive to oversee male-linked behavior because it usually carries higher status and power than female-linked behavior. Social power has strong impact on modeling. Although boys clearly favor male models, when females command power over rewarding resources, boys adopt their behavior. Power, of course, plays a highly influential role in adult pursuits. For example, in the occupational sphere men earn more than women and male-dominated occupations tend to be more highly paid and valued than female-dominated ones. Even on the athletic field, the media is considerably more attentive to, and broadcasts more widely, men's athletic contests than those of women.

Self-monitoring is the first step toward exercising influence over one's behavior but, in itself, such information provides little basis for self-evaluative reactions. Actions give rise to self-reactions through a judgmental function in which the appropriateness of the behavior is evaluated against genderlinked standards and the circumstances under which it occurs. Personal standards are developed from information conveyed by the three principal modes of influence. People form personal standards partly on the basis of how significant persons in their lives have reacted evaluatively to their behavior. Sociological theories of the self tend to emphasize this particular mode of influence. Standards are also drawn from the tutelage of influential persons in one's social environment or from the standards prescribed by them. Advocating certain standards of behavior, even if they are widely shared, does not ensure their adoption. Thus if parents preach gender egalitarianism but model traditional roles, the precepts soon lose their force. Effective tuition requires some social validation through supportive behavioral feedback.

People not only teach and evaluatively prescribe standards for others, they also exemplify them in their evaluative reactions to their own conduct. They respond with self-satisfaction and self-approval when they fulfill their personal standards but negatively when they fall short of, or violate, their standards. Children's own self-evaluative standards are affected by modeled ones to which they have been exposed.

People construct their standards through reflective processing of these multiple sources of direct and vicarious influences, which may vary across individuals and even within individuals in what they practice for themselves and prescribe for others. From such diverse experiences children learn the evaluative significance of gender in a wide variety of contexts. These include familial roles, peer interactions, occupational and leisure pursuits. Added to this diversity is the need to consider the changing and conflicting messages about the value of traditional gender roles. Therefore, the standards people construct for themselves are not merely facsimiles of what they have been taught, evaluatively prescribed, or have seen modeled.

With increasing cognitive capabilities, children become more aware of the variability and diversity of gender role behavior. Widespread cultural changes add further to the heterogeneity and changeability of gender conceptions and standards. When long hair and culinary skill became in vogue for men, those who were adorned with flowing locks and cultivated their cooking skills viewed themselves as masculine as did men with cropped hair who eschewed the kitchen.

Similarly, with the rebirth of the women's movement in the 1960's, women sought to redefine their role beyond homemaking and childcare. Their struggle for equal rights and opportunities has increased the numbers of women entering a wide variety of occupations including male dominated ones. Although the workforce remains extensively gender segregated and men tend to dominate the higher status positions, it now is more acceptable for women to combine occupational pursuits with family responsibilities through choice rather than need. Judgments of one's behavior against personal standards sets the occasion for self-reactive influence. Self-evaluative reactions provide the mechanism through which standards regulate courses of action. Self-approving reactions for behavior that measures up to personal standards, and self-censure for behaving in ways that violate those standards give direction to behavior and provide motivators for it. Both gender constancy and gender schema theory emphasize conception matching as the primary regulative process.

Social cognitive theory posits both the standard-matching function and the motivating self-reactive function. Research conducted in different domains reveal that both functions are necessary in the motivation and regulation of conduct. The power of self-reactive regulation has been verified in major domains of functioning including academic development; creativity; health behavior; organizational functioning; transgressive conduct; and aggressive patterns of behavior. The regulative role of self-reactive influence through personal standards in gender-related behavior will be examined in sections that follow. After self-regulatory capabilities have been developed, behavior usually produces two sets of outcomes: self-evaluative reactions and social reactions. They may operate as complementary or as opposing influences on behavior. The way in which gender roles are orchestrated is largely determined by the interplay between personal and social sources of influence.

In the agentic sociocognitive view, people are self-organizing, proactive, selfreflective, and self-regulating not just reactive organisms shaped and shepherded by external events. The capacity to exercise control over one's thought processes, motivation, affect and action operates through mechanisms of personal agency. Among the mechanisms of agency, none is more central or pervasive than people's beliefs in their capabilities to produce given levels of attainments. Unless people believe they can produce desired effects by their actions they have little incentive to act or to persevere in the face of difficulties. Perceived efficacy is, therefore, the foundation of human agency.

Developmental analyses reveal that perceived self-efficacy is a common pathway through which different forms of social influence affect the quality of human functioning throughout the life course. People's beliefs in their efficacy can be developed in four major ways. The most effective way of instilling a strong sense of efficacy is through graded mastery experiences. Successes build a robust belief in one's personal efficacy. Failures undermine it. A resilient sense of efficacy requires experience in overcoming obstacles through perseverant effort. The second way of creating and strengthening selfefficacy is by social modeling. Models transmit knowledge, skills and strategies for managing environmental demands. Seeing people similar to oneself succeed by sustained effort raises observer's beliefs in their own capabilities. The failures of others instill self-doubts about one's own ability to master similar activities.

Social persuasion is the third mode of influence. Expressing faith in people's capabilities raises their beliefs that they have what it takes to succeed. But effective efficacy builders do more than convey positive appraisals. They structure activities in ways that bring success and do not place people prematurely in situations likely to bring failure. People also rely partly on inferences from their physical and emotional states in judging their capabilities. The fourth way of modifying efficacy beliefs is to reduce people's stress and depression, build their physical strength and change misinterpretations of their physical states. Efficacy beliefs exert their effects through their impact on cognitive, motivational, and affective processes and on selection of activities and environments. Perceived personal efficacy influences the choices people make, their aspirations, how much effort they mobilize in a given endeavor, how long they persevere in the face of difficulties and setbacks, whether their thought patterns are selfhindering or self-aiding, the amount of anxiety and stress they experience in coping with taxing and threatening environments, their vulnerability to depression, and their resilience to adversity.

Efficacy beliefs play a pivotal role in the exercise of personal agency because they not only operate on behavior in their own right, but through their impact on other classes of motivators. The effects of goals, outcome expectations, causal attributions, and perceived environmental opportunities and impediments on motivation are partly governed by beliefs of personal efficacy. The outcomes people anticipate depend largely on their beliefs of how well they can perform in given situations. Those of high efficacy expect to gain favorable outcomes; those who expect poor performances of themselves conjure up negative outcomes. It is partly on the basis of efficacy beliefs that people choose what goal challenges to undertake, how much effort to invest in the endeavor, and how long to persevere in the face of difficulties. When faced with obstacles, setbacks, and failures, those who doubt their abilities slacken their efforts, give up, or settle for mediocre solutions. Those who have a strong belief in their abilities redouble their effort to master the challenges. Efficacy beliefs influence causal attributions. People who regard themselves as highly efficacious ascribe their failures to insufficient effort, inadequate strategies, or unfavorable circumstances. Those of low efficacy attribute their failures to low ability. Efficacy beliefs also play an influential role in how formidable obstacles appear. People of high perceived efficacy view impediments as surmountable; those of low efficacy view them as daunting obstacles over which they can exert little control. In judging their environmental circumstances, people who are assured in their efficacy focus on the opportunities worth pursuing rather than dwell on risks, and take a future time perspective in structuring their lives.

Research in diverse activity domains has furthered understanding of how efficacy beliefs enable children and adults to contribute to their accomplishments and well-being through the exercise of selfregulatory influences. People are partly the product of their environment. Hence, they can also have a hand in what they become by the types of activities they choose to get into. In efficacy guided self-development through choice processes, personal destinies are shaped by selection of environments known to cultivate valued potentialities and lifestyles. The power of efficacy beliefs to affect the life paths of men and women through selection processes is most clearly revealed in studies of career choice and development. Occupational choices are of considerable importance because they structure a major part of people's everyday reality, provide them with a source of personal identity and determine their satisfaction and the quality of their worklife. Efficacy beliefs set the slate of options for serious consideration. For example, people rapidly eliminate from consideration entire classes of vocations on the basis of perceived efficacy, regardless of the benefits they may hold. Those who have a strong sense of personal efficacy consider a wide range of career options, show greater interest in them, prepare themselves better for different careers and have greater staying power in their chosen pursuits. Occupational pursuits are extensively gendered.

The pervasive stereotypic practices of the various societal subsystems eventually leave their mark on women's beliefs about their occupational efficacy. Male students have a comparable sense of efficacy for both traditionally male-dominated and female-dominated occupations. In contrast, female students judge themselves more efficacious for the types of occupations traditionally held by women, but have a weaker sense of efficacy that they can master the educational requirements and job functions of traditionally male gendered occupations, even though they do not differ in actual verbal and quantitative ability. The disparity in perceived efficacy for male-dominated and female-dominated occupations is greatest for women who view themselves as highly feminine, distrust their quantitative capabilities, and believe there are few successful female models in traditionally male-dominated occupations. Although efficacy beliefs contribute more heavily to occupational preferences than beliefs about the benefits attainable by different pursuits, women base their occupational preferences even more heavily on their perceived efficacy than on the potential benefits the vocations yield.

Gender differences disappear, however, when women judge their efficacy to perform the same activities in everyday situations in stereotypically feminine tasks than in the context of male-dominated occupations. Such findings suggest that gender related efficacy impediments arise from stereotype linkage rather than actual capabilities. Gender stereotyping of pursuits that suggests lesser ability diminishes judgments of personal efficacy. Women's beliefs about their capabilities and their career aspirations are shaped by undermining social practices within the family, the educational system, peer relationships, the mass media, the occupational system, and the culture at large. Because quantitative abilities are an essential entry skill for scientific and technical occupations, a low sense of mathematical self-efficacy operates as a major barrier to a whole range of occupational pursuits requiring quantitative skills.

Gender affects perceived mathematical efficacy through mathematical preparation in high school, mathematical achievement, and masculine gender-role orientation. Masculine gender-role orientation and level of mathematical achievement foster math-related educational and career choices through their effects on perceived mathematical efficacy rather than directly. Perceived mathematical efficacy promotes selection of mathematically-orientated educational and career pursuits both directly and by lowering vulnerability to anxiety over mathematical activities. Gender and prior mathematical preparation also have a direct effect on choice of academic major. As in selection of quantitatively-oriented course work, the effect of gender on mathematical performance is mediated through perceived self-efficacy rather than operates directly. Simply invoking the gender stereotype can undermine women's efficacy to make good use of the mathematical competencies they possess. Women's lowered sense of mathematical efficacy is, of course, changeable. Mastery experiences eliminate gender differences.

Computer systems are playing an increasing role in educational development and serving as a major information management and decision-making tool in the modern workplace. Through their association with mathematics and electronic technology, computers have become masculinized. As a result, boys receive encouragement from an early age by parents and teachers to develop computer literacy. As a consequence, they regard computer skills as more important to their career development than do girls. Societal practices that breed perceived inefficacy in the use of computer tools is thus creating new occupational impediments for women. Even at an early age, girls express a lower sense of computer efficacy than do boys. Gender differences in perceived computer efficacy extend to the college level as well. Those of low perceived efficacy show less interest in acquiring computer competencies, are less inclined to pursue computer coursework and see computer literacy as less relevant to their future careers. Thus, men are benefiting much more than women from these technological advancements.

In focusing on the influential role of perceived efficacy in gender differences in career aspirations and pursuits one should not lose sight of the earlier discussion that cultural constraints, inequitable incentive systems, and truncated opportunity structures shape women's career development. These social realities form an important part of the triadic model of causation. It should also be noted that the variability within sexes exceeds the differences between them. Therefore, modal sex characteristics in perceived efficacy should not be imputed to all members within each sex group. Indeed, women who take a more egalitarian view toward the role of women display a higher sense of efficacy for traditionally male occupations and are more oriented toward such careers in high school and pursue them in college. They construct different identities and futures for themselves. Perceived self-efficacy predicts career nontraditionality.

The self-efficacy component of social cognitive theory does more than identify a contributory factor to career development. The theory provides the means for enhancing the personal source of control over the course of one's self-development. For example, at the elementary school level, girls mathematical self-efficacy and skills can be raised to the level of boys by guided mastery experiences. Similarly, at the occupational level, programs combining modeling with enabling feedback, build perceived self-efficacy and skill in using financial software for varied business functions in women who harbored strong self-doubts about their efficacy to use computerized systems. The same set of factors posited by social cognitive theory to explain and predict behavior inform and guide effective interventions as well across diverse spheres of functioning. Gender differences are also evident in the way in which beliefs of personal efficacy affect emotional well-being. For example, women are generally more prone to depression than men, a difference that emerges in late adolescence. Because of its prevalence and impairment of functioning, children's depression can have an important impact on the course of gender development.

Perceived inefficacy to control things one values contributes to depression in several ways.

One route is through unfulfilled aspirations. People

who impose on themselves standards of self-worth they judge they cannot attain drive themselves to depression.

A second route to depression is through a low sense of social efficacy to develop social relationships that bring satisfaction to one's life and make chronic stressors easier to bear. Social support, in turn, produces beneficial effects only to the extent that it raises perceived coping efficacy.

The third route to depression is through control efficacy. Much human depression is cognitively generated by dejecting, ruminative thought.

A low sense of efficacy to control ruminative thought contributes to the occurrence, duration and recurrence of depressive episodes. Microanalyses reveal that the self-efficacy pathways to childhood depression differ across gender. A low sense of social efficacy contributes more heavily to depression in girls than in boys. Moreover, girls are more likely to get depressed over beliefs about academic inefficacy even though they surpass their male counterparts in their academic work. Gender differences also appear in perceived efficacy for affect regulation. A strong sense of efficacy to manage positive emotions is accompanied by high prosocialness similarly for males and females. In contrast, a low sense of efficacy to manage negative emotions is highly depressing for females but not for males.

The heavier involvement of social and affective facets of perceived self-efficacy for girls may help to explain their greater proneness to depression in late adolescence and adulthood. Preexisting perceived self-inefficacy in more aspects of their lives make it more difficult to manage heightened transitional stressors and new role demands without experiencing despondency.

Social cognitive theory extends the analysis of human agency to collective agency. Personal and collective efficacy differ in the unit of agency but both forms of efficacy beliefs serve similar functions and operate through similar processes. People's shared beliefs in their efficacy influence the type of futures they seek to achieve collectively; how much effort they put into their group endeavors; their staying power when collective efforts fail to produce quick results or meet forcible opposition; their vulnerability to discouragement, and the social changes they are able to realize. Beneficial gender role development is a social matter not just a personal one. Handicapping practices that are built into the social order require social remedies. The collective social efforts must address the expectations, belief systems, and social practices in the home, school, mass media and the workplace that not only diminish personal efficacy and aspirations but erect institutional impediments to making the most of one's talents. The exercise of collective efficacy for social and policy initiatives is aimed at raising public awareness of inequitable practices, educating and influencing policymakers and mobilizing public support for warranted social changes.

Women gained voting rights after a prolonged struggle through the forcible collective action of the Women's Suffrage Movement. In contemporary efforts in the political arena, through the organized collective power of its political network, Emily's List is elevating women to positions of legislative power by providing financial support, building winning campaigns, and mobilizing women voters.

Gender Development

The earlier analyses of extant conceptions of gender development document the need for an alternative theory of gender development and functioning. To recap briefly the major conceptual and empirical problems, although gender identity and constancy were posited as the factors governing gender development, the mechanisms by which they come into being remain unspecified. They are simply assumed to be products of interaction with the environment. However, this deficiency is the least of the problems because it is conceptually remediable. The nonpredictiveness of the posited cognitive factors seriously question the viability of the major tenets of the theories themselves. Neither gender identity, gender constancy, nor gender stereotypic knowledge predicts gender-linked conduct. Young children exhibit preferences long before they acquire gender conceptions or understand the gender linkage of their preferences. Nor does knowledge of gender stereotypes predict gender-linked conduct in older children or adults. Virtually all of them know the stereotypes but vary in their behavior.

Cognitive-developmental and schema theories posited knowledge of gender identity or constancy as the intrapsychic automotivator of gender-linked conduct. That is, attainment of gender self-knowledge leads one to emulate and do "girls things" or "boy things". The behavioral nonpredictiveness of gender self-knowledge alone calls into question the regulatory tenets of the theory as well. Clearly, other motivational and regulatory mechanisms govern gender-linked conduct. Differentiation of gender roles is a sociostructural phenomenon, rather than merely an intrapsychic one. Human development and functioning operate within a broad network of social influences rather than within a socially insulated cognitivism. If doing "girl things" and "boy things" had no differential social effects gender labeling would lose its significance. Gender typing remains highly salient because it makes a big difference in one's life experiences. The constellation of gender attributes and roles people adopt are socially propagated matter not just an intrapsychic one. Sociostructural theories and psychological theories are often viewed as rival conceptions of human behavior or as representing different levels of causation. Human functioning cannot be fully understood solely in terms of sociostructural factors or psychological factors.

A full understanding requires an integrated perspective in which social influences operate through psychological mechanisms to produce behavioral effects. When analyzed within a unified causal structure, sociostructural influences produce behavioral effects largely through self processes rather than directly. The effects of sociostructural influences on the functioning of social systems are also in large part mediated through the collective agency of the operators of the systems.

During the first year of life infants can distinguish between the two sexes and by the second year they engage in gender-linked conduct and prefer activities associated with their own gender. Because gender is such a significant category for societal organization, it takes on special importance from birth. Children learn to categorize people on the basis of their gender from a very early age. By 7 months infants can discriminate between male and female faces and between male and female voices. Hair length and voice pitch are distinguishing features for such discriminations. By 9 months, infants begin to show intermodal gender knowledge. When presented with pairs of male and female pictures they attend more to female faces when they hear female voices, and by 12 months they attend more to male than female faces when they hear male voices. Consider the pervasive social forces that are brought to bear on the development of gender orientation from the very beginning of life. Parents do not suspend influencing gender orientations until children can identify themselves as girls and boys. On the contrary, parents begin the task at the very outset of development. They do so by the way they structure the physical environment and by their social reactions around activities. From the moment of birth, when infants are categorized as either male or female, many of the social influences that impinge on them are determined by their gender. Parents reveal strong gendered beliefs about their newborns even when there are no objective differences in size or activity. Parents of newborn girls rate them as finer featured, weaker, softer, and more delicate than parents of newborn boys. For most children, both their physical and social environments are highly gendered. Names, clothing, and decoration of infants' rooms are all influenced by their categorization as either female or male. Boys are adorned in blue and girls in pink. Boys are attired in rugged trousers, girls in pastel jeans or skirts. They are given different hair styles as well. Children come to use differential physical attributes, hair styles, and clothing as indicants of gender. Much early role learning occurs in play. The forms play takes are structured and channeled by social influences.

Parents stereotypically stock their sons' rooms with educational materials, machines, vehicles, and sports equipment, and their daughters' rooms with baby dolls, doll houses, domestic items, and floral furnishings. Boys are provided with a greater variety of toys than girls.

These play materials orient boys' activities and interests to gender roles usually performed outside the home. By contrast, girls are given toys directed toward domestic roles such as homemaking and child care. Parents are also more likely to purchase gender-traditional than gender-nontraditional toys requested by their children. The amount of time spent playing with toys traditionally linked to one's gender or the other gender is highly related to the types of toys parents provide. Thus, the gender-linked play materials arranged for children channels their spontaneous play into traditionally feminine or masculine roles.

The differentiation of the sexes extends beyond the realm of attire, make-believe play, and other playful activities. Whenever appropriate occasions arise, parents and others instruct children in the kinds of behavior expected of girls and boys and provide evaluative feedback when it is performed. Mothers respond more negatively when their children engage in gender-atypical than gender typical activities. Although not all parents are inflexible gender stereotypers in all activities, most accept, model, and teach the sex roles traditionally favored by the culture. Social sanctions bear heavily on gender-linked conduct even in the earliest years. Parents convey to their children positive and negative sanctions through affective reactions and evaluative comments. Affective communication through intonation patterns, smiles and frowns are highly salient events that direct infant's behavior when their verbal skills are limited. Positive affective reactions promote approach behavior, whereas negative affective reactions promote avoidant forms of behavior. For preverbal children, the intonation of maternal comments has more impact on their behavior than does the semantic content.

Although preverbal children cannot label their own sex or that of others or even the gender linkage of objects, parental affective reactions and communications about the objects are sufficient to sway their children's play. Parents are excited, smile, and comment approvingly when their children engage in activities considered appropriate for their gender, but they are likely to show and voice disapproval when their children take up activities deemed appropriate for the other gender. These affective reactions, depending on their nature, create positive and negative orientations to gender-linked objects and activities. These findings are in accord with a great deal of evidence from other spheres of functioning on parental affective regulation of children's approach and avoidance reactions to ambiguous and novel objects. Modeled affective reactions not only shape behavioral orientations but alter the valence of the activities themselves. Objects and activities thus get gendered through such reactive, instructive, and modeled social means.

Even during the early years, fathers are more stereotypic socializers than are mothers. The father's intonation probably alerted the child to avoid the "masculine" toys as much as what he said. Starting in infancy and continuing through to middle childhood, fathers are more encouraging of physically active play for sons than for daughters. Apart from parental evaluative reactions and direct tutelage concerning gender-linked conduct, children also notice the various activities modeled by their parents and peers. Modeling influences are important even in children's early gender development. Because gender is a category carrying consequential outcomes, girls attend closely to female models and boys to male models before they can label themselves or others according to gender. The ability to differentiate the two sexes and to link them to different activities and their associated social sanctions is all that is necessary for children to begin to learn gender-role stereotypes. The children choose activities consistent with gender-linked stereotypes from having observed certain activities occur correlatively with the two sexes before they have a conception of gender. This level of gender understanding precedes gender self-identity which already involves abstraction of a set of gender attributes integrated into a more general knowledge structure. When exposed to a female model engaging in male-and female-stereotyped activities, boys of 25 months emulated male-stereotyped activities to a greater extent than female-stereotyped ones. In contrast, girls of this age showed no differential emulation of the female—and male-stereotyped sequences. Evidently, the stronger gender-typing pressures for boys leads them to favor male-stereotypical activities, even before they had acquired gender stereotypical knowledge.

As children become more cognitively adept, their knowledge of gender extends beyond nonverbal categorization of people and objects, to explicit labeling of people, objects, and styles of behavior according to gender. As children begin to comprehend speech, they notice that verbal labeling in masculine and feminine terms is used extensively by those around them. It does not take them long to learn that children are characterized as boys and girls, and adults as mothers and fathers, women and men. Gender labeling gives salience not only to sorting people on the basis of gender but also aggregates the features and activities that characterize each gender. It not only highlights gender as an important category for viewing the world, but as the basis for categorizing oneself. Once such self-categorization occurs the label takes on added significance, especially as children increasingly recognize that the social world around them is heavily structured around this categorical differentiation.

One's gender status makes a big difference. It carries enormous significance not only for dress and play, but the skills cultivated, the occupations pursued, the functions performed in family life, and the nature of ones leisure pursuits and social relationships. Social cognitive theory posits that, through cognitive processing of direct and vicarious experiences, children come to categorize themselves as girls or boys, gain substantial knowledge of gender attributes and roles, and extract rules as to what types of behavior are considered appropriate for their gender. However, unlike the gender constancy and schema theories, it does not invest gender conceptions with automatic directive and motivating properties. Acquiring a conception of gender and valuing the attributes defining that conception are separable processes governed by different determinants. In the preceding sections have seen how self-regulatory mechanisms operate through perceived self-efficacy, anticipated social sanctions, self-sanctions, and perceived impediments rather than gender labeling itself motivating and guiding gender-linked conduct. Just as having a conception of one's own gender does not drive one to personify the stereotype it embraces, nor does the self-conception of gender necessarily create positive valuation of the attributes and roles traditionally associated with it.

Both the valuation of certain attributes and roles and the eagerness to adopt them are influenced by the value society places on them. Societies that subordinate women may lead many of them to devalue their own gender identity. Boys clearly favor male models, but girls, who are fully cognizant of their gender constancy, do not display the exclusive same-gender modeling as the cognitivistic theories would have one believe. For boys there is little conflict between their own valuation of their gender and societal valuation of it. For girls, however, although they may value being a girl and gender-linked activities, they very early recognize the differential societal valuation of male and female roles. Consequently, women have some incentive to attempt to raise their status by mastering activities and interests traditionally typed as masculine. Even at the preschool level, girls show greater modeling after the other gender than do boys.

In the social sphere, there are large gender differences in the modeling of aggression, which is widely regarded as a principal attribute of maleness. The heavy aggressive modeling by males is not lost on boys. Even at the very early age preschool boys are higher adopters of modeled styles of aggression than girls, and even more so if it is modeled by males than by females. Although boys are more inclined than girls to adopt modeled aggressive styles of behavior, the differences reflect primarily differential restraint rather than differential acquisition. When girls are offered positive incentives to reproduce the novel patterns of aggression they saw modeled, the results show that girls learn just about as much as boys from the aggressive models. The basic messages they convey shape public images of reality. In the gendered portrayals of aggression in adult relationships, men are usually the aggressors, whereas women are more often helpless victims. When women do aggress, they are more likely to get punished for it than are men.

In the televised world, men wield aggressive power extensively, but in the everyday world most people do

3

Behavioural Outcome and Perceptual Features

Several researches on family relationships and behavioral outcome have revealed tahat many family characteristics are believed to be responsible for changes in a child's psychological reaction to family stress. Having positive relationships with family members, opportunities for personal growth within the family and the provision of structure have been proposed as possible protective factors. Having a good relationship with at least one parent has been shown to significantly reduce the amount of maladaptive behavior in children who had experienced family discord. Although the exploration of the presence or absence of family protective factors may contribute to the understanding of the relationship between exposure to stressful family events and behavioral outcomes, other constructs might also be influential.

By classifying children according to their family stress exposure only, it is not possible to determine each individual's unique experience of life events. It is probable, that not all children would perceive any single event as equally negative. Therefore, some children might adapt well after an event if seen as mild or positive, and other children would develop serious psychopathology after exposure to the same event if perceived as intensely negative. The appraisal or interpretation of an event may influence the coping resources the child implements when a family stress event occurs. However, when stress exposure is measured as a "presence or absence" variable, it is not possible to detect the influence of individual interpretation. Given that the relation between stress exposure and maladjustment is often a modest one, the importance of interpretation of the stressful event in contributing to adjustment has received more examination.

Several researchers have suggested that a child's perception of major life events can significantly influence behavior and adjustment. The term primary appraisal to reflect the beliefs an individual has about the personal significance of events. Within this construct, he identified three components:

a) ego involvement,

b) goal relevance, and goal congruence.

Several studies have explored various dimensions of the three components, suggesting that children appraise the same event differently and it is this notion of appraisal that might lead to debilitating or protective effects. For example, Smith and Brodzinsky found that adopted children who had a negative appraisal of being adopted had more maladjustment and avoidant coping styles than children with more positive appraisals of adoption. Furthermore, in a longitudinal study of children exposed to divorce, found that negative appraisal of divorce was predictive of anxiety symptoms over and above the direct effects of the divorce stress itself. Similarly, it was children's negative appraisal of their parents' cancer, and not the actual stage and prognosis of the disease, that was predictive of anxiety and depressive symptoms in children. Similarly, some investigators have suggested that children who tend to interpret stress events positively may be more likely to adapt effectively after the event. For example, children who experienced little social support but who appraised the events they experienced as positive displayed less internalizing and externalizing behavior as these life events increased than did children with significantly higher support and less positive ratings of stress events.

The results suggested that positive appraisal might act as a potential protective factor for children with lower levels of other protective factors. This is an important contrast to the conclusions in research on adults, which indicate that positively endorsed life events are relatively unrelated to behavioral outcome. However, the role of a child's perception of family events in relation to the presence of other known family characteristics and behavioral outcomes is still unclear. It is not enough to simply understand that there is a relationship among the constructs of family stress, family dynamics, and behavioral outcomes. It is necessary to investigate the mechanisms of this relation. To determine a buffering or nonbuffering outcome, researchers must include a comprehensive behavioral outcome focus. By including both adaptive and maladaptive behavior, specific comparisons between different types of maladjustment and adjustment can be made.

Family factors and appraisal appear to play a role in the prediction of behavioral outcomes for children exposed to family stress events. To date, however, no study has included a focus on the role of appraisal and family factors for children exposed to family life events. Past research has suggested that both positively appraised events and the presence of protective factors operate to enhance adaptive behavior. Furthermore, negatively appraised events and the absence of protective factors may lead to greater internalizing and externalizing symptoms. Therefore, it was predicted that children with high levels of positive family environment characteristics who reported a large amount of family life events as positive would exhibit high levels of adaptive behavior and low levels of maladaptive symptoms. It was also predicted that the reverse would be true for children with low levels of positive family environmental characteristics and negative endorsement of their family life events.

Family Relationships and Behavioral Outcome: Experimental Analysis

A study conducted in Europe to test these predictions illustrate the relationships among exposure to family events, appraisal of these events, family characteristics, and behavioral outcome. Participants were 260 children between the ages of 8 and 12 years, with a mean age of 10.80 years. Forty-nine percent were boys, and all children were students in general classrooms at several schools in a semirural town. The ethnic and socioeconomic background of the sample was representative of children in the target area. Specifically, 86.4% of the participants were European Americans, and 17% of the sample were classified in the lower socioeconomic status, 54% in the middle socioeconomic status, and 29% in the upper socioeconomic status using

Duncan's Revised Socio-Economic Index.

Family life events: Family life events were measured by the Life Events Checklist (LEC). The LEC is a self-report measure consisting of a list of 46 events likely to be experienced by young people (e.g., moving to a new home, experiencing illness in the family, making the honor roll, being suspended from school). Children indicated how many of the listed events they had experienced in the past year and then indicated if they felt those specific events were positive or negative. For the study, only those items that were related to family experiences or family members were included, making 18 family stress events possible. From this measure, two scores were calculated. The Negative Family Stress score was the total number of events endorsed by the child as negative, and the Positive Family Stress score was the total number of events endorsed by the child as positive. The number of family life events endorsed overall was consistent with other studies of elementary school-age children. Several studies have yielded preliminary support for the reliability and validity of the LEC as a measure of the number of life events experienced by children.

Family protective factors (FES) : Family protective factors were measured by the Family Environment Scale. The FES is a 90-item, true/ false questionnaire that provides an assessment of the family environment. Although children age 11 and older can complete this measure, child on this measure would have excluded more than half of the sample. The FES assesses environmental characteristics of families within three broad domains, composed of 10 component subscales. The first domain is the family relationship (FR) domain, which is composed of the cohesion, expressiveness, and conflict subscales. The second domain is the personal growth (PG) domain, which is composed of the independence, achievement orientation, intellectual-cultural orientation, active-recreational orientation, and moral-religious emphasis subscales. The third domain is the system maintenance (SM) domain, which is composed of the organization and control subscales. Total scores in each of the three domains were used as protective factor scores, resulting in three family protective factor scores. The FES has been demonstrated as a useful measure for identifying characteristics important in the psychological adaptation of family members.

Psychosocial adaptation: The child's adaptive, emotional, and behavioral functioning was measured by parent on the Behavior Assessment System for Children (BASC). The BASC is a 148-item, Likert scale measure designed to assess three domains: adaptive, externalizing, and internalizing behavior for children 4 to 18 years old. The adaptive skill domain is composed of four subscales: adaptability, leadership, social skills, and study skills. The externalizing domain is composed of three scales: aggression, hyperactivity, and conduct problems. The internalizing behaviour composite is also made up of three subscales: anxiety, depression, and somatization.

Children and parents from several elementary schools were sent information about the study. Parents who were interested in participating were instructed to return the recruitment form to the child's school. Prospective participants were asked to meet the investigator or one of several graduate research assistants at a prearranged public location (e.g., community center, local church building) to complete the study measures on a weekend. Parents were compensated $5.00 for their participation, and children were given a small toy. Of the 402 parents who received information about the study, 271 (67.4%) of these completed study measures.

The study measures are not appropriate for children whose intelligence levels fall in the mentally retarded range. Therefore, of the 271 potential participants, 11 children were later omitted from the participant pool because their scores on an intelligence-screening tool indicated an intelligence estimate in the mentally retarded range. Therefore, 260 parents and children formed the participant pool for the study. Parents and children completed an informed consent or assent form and then the study measures in random order.

Specifically, adaptive behaviour was negatively correlated with externalizing, internalizing, and each of the two family stress scores (negative and positive). In addition, several of the family characteristic scales were significantly, positively correlated with each other. Surprisingly, the Personal Growth scale was negatively correlated with adaptive behaviour. The potential family protective factor scales were not significantly correlated with the three family stress scores. Although not presented, age was not significantly correlated with the study variables. Furthermore, while gender and socioeconomic status were modestly correlated with adaptive and externalizing behaviour, they were not significantly correlated with the predictor variables. Because of the lack of significant correlations correlations with predictor variables, age, gender, and socioeconomic status were not included in subsequent analyses. Hierarchical regression analyses were conducted to test for main effects and interactions of the two family stress scores (negative and positive) and the three potentially protective family scales to determine how these variables predicted outcome behaviour. To allow for comparison between the outcomes for each of the family stress scores, separate analyses were conducted for each of the stress scores.

The first series of hierarchical analyses used scores on the Adaptive behaviour scale of the BASC as the criterion variable and the two family event scores and the three family environment scores as independent variables. In separate analyses, the results indicated significant main effects for the Personal Growth, Negative, and Positive Family Events scores. These results indicated a consistent pattern in that adaptive behaviour decreased as Negative and Positive Family Events scores increased. In contrast, adaptive behaviour increased as the Personal Growth protective factor increased. The predictor variables, including the negatively rated events, accounted for 4.6% of the variance, and the positively rated events accounted for 5.2% of the variance in adaptive behaviour. In the second step of the regression analyses, interaction parameters were entered into the equations. The regression equations, including interaction terms, did not represent a significant increase from the variance accounted for by the main effects only model.

The second set of hierarchical regression analyses included scores on the Externalizing Behaviour scale of the BASC as the criterion variable. Significant main effects were found for the Negative Family Events score. The results indicated that as Negative Family Stress increased, so did externalizing behaviour. The predictor variables, including the negatively rated events, accounted for 4.4% of the variance, and the positively rated events accounted for 1.8% of the variance in externalizing behaviour. Also, the variance accounted for when interaction parameters were entered into the equations did not represent a significant increase from the variance accounted for by the main effects-only models. In the third set of analyses, the Internalizing Behaviour scale of the BASC was used as the criterion variable. In contrast to the results of the prior analyses, the results indicated no significant main effects for any independent variable scores. However, when interaction terms were added to the equations, two significant interactions were found between the FR and PG scales and the Negative Family Events scores.

As negative family events increased, children in the low FR group demonstrated a consistent decrease in internalizing behaviour; however, children in the high FR group demonstrated a consistent increase in internalizing behaviour. In the second interaction, as negative family stress increased, children in both the high and low PG groups demonstrated an increase in internalizing behaviour. However, the children in the high PG group demonstrated a consistent and significantly higher level of internalizing behaviour than the children in the low PG group.

The lack of support for positive appraisal suggests that positive interpretation was not solely sufficient to boost adaptive functioning or externalizing behaviour after exposure to family stress events. However, this unpredicted result may have been due to the relatively low percentage of children who rated family stress events as positive. Recent preliminary research, however, suggests that perceiving life events as positive may act as a protective factor or a buffer for children who possess inadequate social support. It is likely that appraisal is a multifaceted construct requiring greater complexity of measurement beyond a positive or negative rating. Therefore, the construct of appraisal may require expansion to include a more direct investigation of specific components of the appraisal process. However, the results supported the notion that behavioral outcome is not interchangeable and that different types of behaviour need to be considered separately. The results of the analyses on internalizing behaviour clearly supported this contention and suggested a new direction for the field.

The results revealed two interactions in the prediction of internalizing behaviour. Although statistically significant, the actual variance accounted for by theses relations was small (6.2%). This unexpected finding could be explained by several conclusions. Research has suggested that in addition to the family's characteristics, other factors, such as the child's temperament, intelligence, and social support, could be operating to influence the psychological and behavioral health of the child exposed to family life events. It is also possible that appraisal adds only a small but key component in the interplay between life events, protective factors, and behavioral outcome. However, the importance of empirical results is not solely determined by the mathematical robustness of the findings. Equally important is clinical significance, and the current findings are unprecedented and have considerable implications for children with emotional and behavioral problems. Specifically, the results suggest that for children exposed to family events endorsed as negative, having stronger, more positive family relationships and higher levels of personal development actually serves to increase the amount of internalizing symptomatology.

This is hardly considered a "protective" pattern and in fact suggests that these constructs are more aptly named vulnerability factors for children endorsing family events as negative. These two variable interactions may seem somewhat counter-intuitive. Although this may initially raise some questions about the measures used in the study, all of the measures are accepted ones commonly used to address the similar research questions. Thus, some alternative explanations are in order. Children with less positive family relationships are more likely to demonstrate a decrease in internalizing behaviour as negatively endorsed family stress events increase.

For children with lower levels of personal growth, the result is simply lower amounts of internalizing behaviour as negative family events increase. For these children, having less meaningful relationships with family members may actually serve to diminish anxious or depressive symptoms when negatively perceived family events occur. Consequently, those children who feel less close to family members or who have a reduced sense of personal growth may feel less threatened when major family transitions occur. Although it is unlikely that any clinician would consider a negative family environment as a protective factor, the results of the present study suggest that less personal growth and less positive family relationships may actually have a positive influence in certain contexts.

One of the significant contributions of the current studies is the attempt to question some of the assumptions in the field. Specifically, the uniformity of family events and characteristics implicit in past research appears to be an inaccurate description of what actually occurs. Challenging the notion that because something "sounds" protective that it actually is, calls into question prior suppositions regarding how positive family relations and personal growth advancement actually operate within the family. Interpretation of these results needs to be made in light of two limitations.

— All of the measures were taken at the same point in time; therefore, causal inference cannot be made. Moreover, it is likely that family stress events occurring over the past 12 months could have an impact on variables later assessed as potential family protective factors. That is, temporal variations could exist in the data that make conclusions preliminary.

— Relatively low numbers of total family stress events were reported. However, these family stress events represent major family events in the past 12 months only, suggesting that overall the present sample experienced a major family event every 4 months. Nevertheless, these results should not be interpreted for children exposed to higher numbers of family stress events.

Also, while multiple-informant data is desirable, the fact that all of the stress variables were child and all of the protective factors and outcome behaviour was parent creates the potential for source bias within the constructs. However, each variable are consistent with the best-accepted practices for assessing life events as well as outcome behaviour. It is important to note, however, that the family stress events endorsed are not simply a list of acute events. Most of the events endorsed represented chronic events, and the experience and subsequent adaptation to these events is likely to be an ongoing process.

Next, a relatively small percentage of the sample rated the family events they experienced as positive. By doing so, the role of positive appraisal and family stress events may not have been fully captured and subsequently limited the information on positive appraisal provided by the study. Clearly, given these limitations, these results need to be replicated. However, these results have important implications for future research. Future work needs to determine if the definition of family stress events affects the predictability of child adjustment.

The study examined the importance of the number of family stress life events in the past year. Just as the action of potential protective factors may be dependent on the type of outcome, it may also be dependent on the duration or intensity of family life events experienced. Although the present results are limited, the findings have potentially important theoretical and clinical implications for children with emotional and behavioral problems.

— Despite common comorbidity and the significant correlation between internalizing and externalizing behavior, outside factors may not influence maladaptive behavior symptoms equally. The discovery that different results were found in the prediction of internalizing, externalizing, and adaptive behavior suggests that maladjustment should not be considered a homogenous construct.

— The context of the behavior may be important to consider. The current results suggest that depressive and anxious symptoms may not necessarily signal a child who has been exposed to a maladjusted family environment. On the contrary, the presence of increasing internalizing behaviors may in fact signal increasing negative family life events for a child who has also had the good fortune to experience life in a positive family environment.

— Differing results with the different domains of positive family environment and appraisal suggest that family environment and appraisal are best conceptualized as multifaceted components.

In three experiments with 164 individuals between 4 and 80 years old, the study examined age-related changes in explicit memory for three perceptual features-item identity, color, and location. In Experiments 1-2, feature recognition was assessed in an incidental learning, gamelike task resembling the game Concentration. In Experiment 3, feature recognition was assessed using a pencil-and-paper task after intentional learning instructions. The form of the explicit memory function across the life span varied with the particular perceptual feature tested and the type of task. Item recognition was excellent at all ages but was significantly poorer for older adults than children, color recognition peaked in late childhood on the gamelike task, and location recognition peaked in early adulthood on the pencil-and-paper task. These findings indicate that performance on explicit memory tests is not a consistent inverted U-shaped function of age across various features. Explicit memory performance depends on what is measured and how.

Although they may express the ideas in different ways, current accounts of memory generally distinguish between more perceptually based, automatic, bottom-up processing and more reflectively based, effortful, top-down processing. These accounts also generally agree that remembering events, sometimes called episodic or explicit memory, is characterized by the phenomenal experience of specific features that comprise the event. Thus, episodic memory depends on encoding multiple features and associations among them. Furthermore, reflective activities contribute to establishing such complex event representations. Many, if not all, of such self-initiated or reflective activities are thought to improve during childhood and decline in normal senescence, yielding an inverted U-shaped function for explicit memory.

The view that explicit memory is a U-shaped function of age is a reiteration of the Jacksonian principle of the development and dissolution of function. This principle states that the last function to develop is the first to disappear after brain damage from injury, disease, or aging, whereas the first function to develop is the last to be affected when an organism undergoes demise. Because explicit memory is widely thought to be late maturing, it should also decline in old age if its developmental course is described by the Jacksonian principle.

The Jacksonian principle in cognitive functioning, citing extensive anecdotal evidence that more recent memories are more vulnerable in disease states and old age. More recent studies with children have repeatedly found that explicit memory performance on recall and recognition tests improves with age. Likewise, numerous studies have found that young adults are superior to healthy, older adults on the same tasks. Considered jointly, the studies appear to support the Jacksonian principle. Most of the studies of memory development with children, however, used verbal materials, raising the possibility that age changes in verbal competence contributed to this result. Some researchers sidestepped this potential problem by testing children with pictorial stimuli. Mitchell found that a meta-analysis over nine developmental studies that used pictorial stimuli and that compared at least two age groups of either children or adults on tests of both explicit and implicit memory. All of the studies of explicit memory in his analysis used recognition tests except two, which used cued-recall tests. Mitchell found large age differences in accuracy that were described by an inverted U-shaped function, with older children performing significantly better than younger children (age range 5 3-12 years) and older adults performing significantly worse than young adults (age range 5 18-71 years). He characterized memory development over the life span in traditional Jacksonian terms: "As the most specialized system, episodic memory is the last to develop fully in childhood. Its unique specialization, however, may also make it the most fragile, and therefore it is the first to go in the course of normal aging".

The notion that explicit memory improves during childhood, peaks in young adulthood, and declines in late adulthood as a mirror image of its order of appearance has been uncritically accepted for more than a decade. Mitchell's meta-analysis, however, was performed over different studies that used different tasks, different stimuli, different metrics, and different instructions.

The study reexamined the validity of the general notion that the pattern of explicit memory over the life span is U-shaped. To this end, assessed the memory of children, young adults, and healthy, older adults for three, isolated perceptual features of events-item identity, color, and location. Because individuals' memory performance was based on information that they had just studied and because they were explicitly asked to select the item or color that they had just seen or to respond to the location where they had previously seen an object, the memory test met the commonly accepted criteria for a test of explicit memory.

In Experiment 1, the study team tested 4- and 5-year-olds on a pictorial gamelike incidental learning task. In Experiment 2, they tested groups of 5- to 72-year-olds on an identical, pictorial version of the same task with an expanded set of materials. In Experiment 3, they gave 10-year-olds the same set of materials but used intentional learning instructions and a pencil-and-paper task that had previously been used to study feature recognition with young and healthy, older adults. In all cases, participants saw colored line drawings of objects located in various cells of an array during study, and then they were tested on their memory for individual features (item, color, or location). Unlike most previous tests with children, the memory tests did not re-present the features that were not being tested (e.g., color information was not present when item information was being tested), and the test did not require that these features had been bound together (e.g., participants did not have to remember that the color "blue" went with the ball).

- Is very young children's explicit memory the same for different, basic perceptual features that are common to many events
- Is the pattern of developmental change previously found in studies of explicit memory also found for each of three basic perceptual features when children and adults of different ages are given explicit memory tests for these features-that is, is the same U-shaped function general across different features
- Is the life-span pattern of explicit memory for these basic perceptual features affected by the nature of the task used to measure it.

Experiment 1: Incidental Explicit Memory Performance

of 4- and 5-year olds

Researchers generally agree that explicit memory performance on recognition, cued-recall, and free-recall tests involves the conscious remembering of a specific, prior study episode. They also assume that explicit memory improves with age from childhood until young adulthood and declines in old age. The inverted U-shaped form of this function over the life span undoubtedly reflects changes in the contribution of many factors, including the speed of processing, attention and its control, strategic skills, motivation, contextual integration, verbal competence, and the neurobiological subsystems that underlie all of these factors. Because most memory studies with children have used verbal materials, developmental changes in verbal competence may have contributed to the observation that explicit memory improves during the childhood period. Some developmental researchers have sought to eliminate this problem by using pictorial stimuli in studies with children.

For example, systematically documented the ability of young children and adults to play the game Concentration, which requires that individuals encode and remember multiple items. In this game, identical items appear on two cards in a deck that is shuffled before the cards are placed face down. Participants turn over and then replace each card, one at a time, until they turn over a card that they recognise as being like one they saw before. If they remember where they saw it, then they retrieve the prior card, striking a match. The object of the game is to strike more matches than the other player. Children's memory performance in this game was actually superior to that of adults. The first to challenge the widely held assumption that explicit memory performance improves with age.

In a study that was also motivated by the observation that very young children rarely erred when playing some found that children's memory performance improved with age for the combination of location information and object identity, but it was age-invariant for individual features.

In two experiments, Schumann-Hengsteler showed line drawings of organized scenes to 4- to 10-year-olds and later asked them to reconstruct the scenes from a pool of items. Children's responses were scored for correctly identified items irrespective of where they were placed, correctly located items irrespective of what item was placed there, and correctly located items (the conjunction of identity and location information). Although item identity and item location were scored separately, in following the task instructions, children were likely attempting to use bound identity and location information to reconstruct the pictures, that is, putting a particular item in the place where they remembered seeing it before.

Unlike Experiment 2 of Schumann-Hengsteler, first experiment was designed to test the ability of 4- and 5-year-olds to recognize item, location, and color features when each of these three perceptual attributes was tested independent of the other two attributes. To accomplish this, The study used a modified version of the Concentration game. The stimulus materials were those that had previously been used to study memory and aging and amnesia, and the procedure was modified to be appropriate for use with young children. As in the Concentration game, children actively interacted with the stimulus materials, reaching successively to each location and lifting a card to reveal the particular colored item concealed beneath it.

During testing, children similarly selected the correct card from an array (item and color feature tests) or reached to the spot on the board and put a sticker on it (location feature test). Because children frequently see monochromatic line drawings, children of both ages would be able to recognize black line drawings of colored line drawings of the familiar objects they had just seen.

Children's Learning was Incidental. That is, they were not told to study either the array or a specific feature, and they also were not told that they would later be asked about the information that they saw. Within 5 min after completing the second trial, children were given a feature recognition test in which they were asked to pick out the items or colors that they had just seen or to put stickers on the squares where they had just seen an object.

Experiment 2: Incidental Explicit Memory Performance

The widespread assumption that explicit memory is an inverted U-shaped function of age is particularly tenuous because different memory tasks have been used with individuals of different ages. The feature recognition performance of the young children in Experiment 1 strongly suggested that children's explicit memory performance depends on what is measured. In Experiment 2, therefore, The study team asked if explicit memory for these same three features (item, color, and location) changes in the commonly assumed manner over the life span. To answer this, they administered exactly the same task to children, young adults, and healthy older adults. The children's ages matched the ages of children who had previously received recognition tests with various pictorial materials and the adults' ages matched those of young and healthy older adults who had previously received recognition tests with the same set of pictorial materials used here.

In contrast to these earlier studies of children, however, here the study assessed memory for features presented individually at the time of testing rather than in combination with other features that had been studied, as in Experiment 1 and Chalfonte and Johnson's study of age-related changes in memory.

Fifty-four children, 30 young adults, and 30 healthy older adults were participants. All were recruited through published news releases and by word-of-mouth and were randomly assigned to one of the three feature test groups (a between-subjects design) as they became available for study. The children ranged in age from 5 to 10 years and included 9 boys and 9 girls with a mean age of 5.25 years (SD 5 .32), 9 boys and 9 girls with a mean age of 7.25 years (SD 5 .25), and 7 boys and 11 girls with a mean age of 10.42 years (SD 5 .37). They were Caucasian (44.44%), Asian (3.70%), African American (9.25%), Hispanic (1.85%), and Not Reported (40.74%). The children's parents had a mean educational attainment of 15.56 years (SD 5 0.95), and their mean rank of socioeconomic status was 66.33 (SD 5 21.22). The young adults were upper-level college students and included 13 males and 17 females with a mean age of 22.83 years (SD 5 1.17). They were Caucasian (83%) and Asian (27%). The older adults were recruited from the local community and included 12 males and 18 females with a mean age of 72.1 years (SD 5 5.21). Their mean level of educational attainment was 11.5 years (SD 5 3.6) and mean rank of socioeconomic status was 47.38 (SD 5 25.74). All were Caucasian.

The study and test materials and the procedure were the same as in Experiment 1 except that the number of items in the study array was increased from 12 to 30, and the number of test items was increased from 16 to 20 (10 old items and 10 new items). Also in Experiment 2, participants were not asked to name the objects or colors, and testing was stopped when an individual had picked 10 items.

Experiment 3: Intentional Explicit Memory Performance

In Experiment 2, the study team used a game like task with children, young adults, and healthy older adults to compare their incidental explicit memory for three perceptual features. The general pattern of results favored the children-not the young adults, as would be predicted by the Jacksonian hypothesis. However, if the pattern of results would be the same under intentional learning conditions using the pencil-and-paper task that Chalfonte and Johnson had previously used with young and healthy older adults. Because the pencil-and-paper task is inappropriate for use with younger children, the study team administered it only to a new group of 10-year-olds and compared their memory performance in this task with their memory performance in the gamelike task in Experiment 2. In addition, they compared the memory performance of young and older adults in the gamelike task from Experiment 2 with the memory performance previously obtained by Chalfonte and Johnson from young and older adults in the pencil-and-paper task.

Cognitive psychologists and cognitive neuroscientists

often treat episodic memory as a single entity, or as reflecting one of two states, rather than as the final, expressed outcome of a number of different types of information and processing factors. This assumption and the Jacksonian (first-in, last-out) principle have led to the widely held but oversimplified conclusion that explicit memory improves during childhood, peaks in adulthood, and declines in old age. The present findings raise questions about this conception of the development of explicit memory. First, the explicit memory function for three different perceptual features over the life span was not universally described by the Jacksonian principle-a first-in, last-out principle. Finally, Chalfonte and Johnson previously found that young adults' recognition of location information on a pencil-and-paper test was superior to that of healthy, older adults after intentional learning instructions.

The study found that 10-year-olds' recognition of location information under the same conditions did not differ from that of Chalfonte and Johnson's older adults but was significantly worse than that of their young adults. Thus, the only indication from the present studies of a finding consistent with the Jacksonian hypothesis and resembling the U-shaped function typically used to describe changes in explicit memory over the life span was for the recognition of location feature information as measured on the pencil-and paper test, which peaked at 19 years under intentional learning instructions.

Taken together with previous findings, these results suggest several points and directions for further research. First, the fact that children's color memory was better than that of adults suggests that the availability of verbal categories does not necessarily help memory under all circumstances The finding that children's color memory was actually hurt by intentional learning instructions, which may invoke inappropriate encoding strategies or strategies that are as yet poorly developed, is consistent with this notion. If so, then there may be other features of experience about which children's incidental memory is actually better than that of adults. Alternatively, children may have better color perception-findings by Kovacs and colleagues suggest that the perception of color peaks at 14 years of age, or color may be more salient to children than to adults (i.e., receive more processing). Incidental memory for location was too poor in all age groups to provide a good assessment of potential changes in memory for location across the life span. However, the fact that both children and older adults were less accurate in intentional location memory than young adults suggests that intentional encoding of location information profits from the types of reflective processing, perhaps including verbal coding (e.g., "a saw is in the upper left corner") or relational processing (e.g., "a saw is above the sun") of items, that presumably develop into young adulthood and become less effective in older adults.

These studies investigated the encoding of feature information as a first step toward clarifying age-related changes in explicit memory. Understanding how features become bound together into complex episodic memories is also critical. These two aspects of episodic memory-memory for features and memories for what features go together often are not clearly separated in the developmental literature. The present findings suggest that:

a) a variety of features may have to be systematically

investigated before it is possible to make general conclusions about developmental trends in feature memory, and

b) a range of possible combinations of features may have to be systematically investigated before general conclusions can be drawn about developmental trends in memory for bound features.

Although children's location memory was poor when it was tested independently of item and/or color information, their location memory is quite good under some circumstances, as when they were cued with item and/or color information in the game Concentration. That is, there may indeed be many situations in which children's memory might be worse than that of adults, but there may also be situations in which it might be no worse, or even better.

There is considerable neuropsychological, human neuroimaging, and animal lesion work implicating both the hippocampal system and frontal regions in explicit memory. There is also evidence that older adults' source memory is disrupted more than their memory for individual features and that this is at least partly a consequence of disrupted feature-binding processes at encoding that are mediated by a frontal-hippocampal circuit. Because the development of the hippocampus and frontal regions continues through childhood and these regions show an increasing chance of neuropathology with age, it seems reasonable to expect explicit memory to assume a Jacksonian, U-shaped function. Nevertheless, even should children turn out to be poorer than young adults at some types of feature binding, the present studies reveal that their memory for some types of individual features is not poorer. Eventually, how features and processing components interact with each other and

4

Information Processing in Child

Infants were incapable of mentally representing physical objects. For Piaget this incapacity was a hallmark of the entire period of infancy, a cognitively primitive stage in which the mind could only grasp that which was currently "present to the senses." The problem with objects is that they are three-dimensional volumes in three-dimensional space. This means, given the laws of physics and probability, that most of the time most of the objects in the world are bound to be out of reach, out of ear shot, and invisible. The odd, idiosyncratic object will cohabit arbitrary, personal sector of time and space but even these will only occasionally emerge into view or come within reach. Despite this unpromising backdrop, we all rapidly converge on identical views concerning the objective and universal nature of physical objects, their mode of existence, their kinds and causal powers, assigning to each an individual and enduring identity. The problem of how this rapid convergence takes place has exercised thinkers for many generations but it is only within the past several decades that we have begun to make real empirical progress. Piaget believed that the key to this problem was the capacity to conceive of objects as enduring through their periods of concealment. The trick was to represent an image of the object to yourself in its absence so as to mimic its continued presence. Bower rejected Piaget's focus on permanence and replaced it with the problem of identity. Even if the young brain can "re-present" an absent object, the deeper problem remains as to how the brain can represent "self-same object" as opposed to merely "similar object." If "re-presenting" is simply a matter of entertaining a mental image or picture of the object, there can be no difference between "self-same one" and "very-similar-looking one."

Recognizing identity for an object carries with it the need to recognize individuality, since the question of identity concerns identity of an individual. Individuality in turn raises the question of how many objects one is dealing with, even if "exactly one" is the answer. The twin problems of object individuation and identity have rightly come to dominate current work on the "object concept." Bower's rejection of the permanence problem received support from the finding that the infant visual system is designed from the bottom up for a 3D world. More especially, it received support from work showing a surprisingly rich set of infant expectations about life behind occluders. Recently, attention has come to focus on infants' ability to individuate objects, both through studies of infant counting and through studies of inferences based on spatiotemporal and property information. Spelke has produced a compelling body of evidence that infants have a fundamental sense of physical objects as discrete, cohesive, bounded volumes that exist in a continuous fashion in time and space. The "Spelke object" derives its unique identity by tracing a unique "world line," to use the physicists' phrase.

Carey and Spelke, the impact of kind concepts on infants' individuation judgements. According to Xu and Carey, the infant begins with only a concept of the Spelke object, undifferentiated with respect to categories. That is, younger infants have the concept, thing, but not, the concepts, BALL or CUP. This means that when the younger infant observes objects emerging from and returning behind an occluder one at a time, the infant has no way of determining how many objects are in the parade. This is because both objects share part of their world lines. This renders the spatiotemporal information ambiguous.

Since the infant cannot determine the distinctness of the world lines, the younger infant cannot determine the distinctness of the objects. Older infants around 12 months, however, have, according to Xu and Carey's account, begun to acquire differentiated kind concepts. Differentiated kind concepts give the older infant a new ability to use the property differences exhibited by the successive objects in the parade to determine their distinctness as individuals. Although the infant had been able to perceive and discriminate the properties for a long time, she was previously unable to infer distinct identity on their basis. Borrowing the philosophical theory of sortals, they propose that a given kind concept provides criteria for how to individuate and identify objects belonging to that kind. The undifferentiated kind concept, thing, provides only criteria referring to spatiotemporal factors. But a differentiated sortal, like Cup, will include criteria referring to other properties of the object, such as shape, by which a cup can be distinguished from a non-cup and be identified as self-same (or different) individual cup. Hence, the older infant, armed with knowledge of the individuation and identity criteria for something being a cup, no longer has to rely upon spatiotemporal factors alone and knows how to count cups when spatiotemporal information is ambiguous.

Xu and Carey's intriguing hypothesis is controversial and has been challenged by results from a number of experiments. These authors have argued that with certain simplified displays, infants as young a 4.5 months will use featural differences to individuate objects, long before the infants in Xu and Carey's experiments. Baillargeon and colleagues agree that when infants are required to make judgements across events involving the removal of an occluder, infants will fail to individuate by feature until around 12 months. But they also argue that if younger infants are required to make judgements about simpler events in which, though an occluder is present, it is never removed, then they can show quite good performance individuating objects by feature. Needham uses events that do not involve full occlusion and do not involve making judgements across events in which an occluder is removed. Arguably then, she uses an "event monitoring" task and finds that young babies can use object features in making individuation judgements.

Framework for Object Tracking

A claim that the younger child lacks a competence is met by a counterclaim that the competence can be detected by more sensitive methods. Determining the competence of a cognitive system at different points in development is a fundamental task of cognitive science and essential if are ever to gain insight into the "mechanisms of development." However, it is seldom possible for us to fruitfully investigate competence without also developing serious ideas regarding performance. By "competence," we mean in this context the representational resources the infant has, the available concepts, regardless of whether or how the infant can actually use those resources in particular situations. By "performance," mean all those factors that enter into determining whether and how the competence is used in particular situations, for example, the nature of working memory, executive functioning, and attention.

We have been developing a theoretical framework that we believe is useful for formulating the different competence and performance aspects of the object concept. The aims in formulating this framework have been twofold: to understand the relation between competence and performance in the object concept and to do so in a way that makes use of ideas that are independently motivated by studies of object cognition in adults. It is always possible that the organization of infant cognitive systems will turn out to be so radically different from that of adults that completely different ideas are needed in the two cases. However, this seems unlikely. A better working assumption is that the major systems present in the adult are the very systems we see developing in the infant. If so, it is useful to align infant and adult studies. One of the most important insights from the study of object cognition in adults is that traditional models which incorporate only sensory processing and longterm memory stores are inadequate.

The traditional model assumes that sensory codes describing the featural properties of an object activates the long-term memory representation best matching that set of features. This long-term representation allows access to more information (e.g., by association or inference) than is contained in the activating feature set. The extra information might include, the kind to which the object belongs, functional information, and, in the case of the adult, the word for this type of object. The activation of a long-term representation identifies the distal object that corresponds to the proximal sensory input. If the sensory input carries "bottom-up" information, then long-term memory provides further information that can be used "top-down." For example, the sensory input from the sight of a dog's head poking out of bushes will bottom-up active a long-term representation, DOG (e.g., by matching a stored visual template of a dog-head).

This activation of DOG makes further information available, e.g., information about tails. The stored and now activated information about dog tails might in turn be used "top-down" to enhance the parsing of the sensory input-so, for example, only now, for the first time, from among the tangle of branches, the dog's tail is discerned. Both Needham and colleagues and Xu and Carey implicitly assume this traditional model. For example, Xu and Carey postulate that long-term stored-object kind concepts (or sortals) are used top-down to individuate and identify objects in sensory input. Kind concepts have to be stored in long-term memory, but, once activated by sensory input, will influence how that input is interpreted. On the other hand, if the infant lacks the appropriate long-term representations, then she will fail to identify the sensory input appropriately and fail to individuate the objects involved.

In addition to sensory codes and iconic memory, on the one hand, and generic object kind representations and long-term memory, on the other, attended objects are also coded episodically and these codes maintained temporarily in working memory. Although there is a wealth of experimental support, the idea is most easily conveyed by the following gedanken offered. Each of these activated long-term representations, BIRD, PLANE, SUPERMAN, is used to refer to the same individual; we experience that individual as maintaining a constant identity despite the succession of radically different descriptions of it that we entertain. So the brain must have some way, other than by long-term generic representations, to refer to and track individuals through particular episodes. An object file indexes a particular individual by way of its locations-through-time without regard to its other properties. A long-term object kind representation is a generic representation. CUP represents the generic category that has cups as members: it does not by itself represent an individual. To represent an individual, CUP requires something additional, for example, a quantifier like "a" or "the" to represent a cup or the cup. Even a quantified long-term representation like this does not yet refer to a specific individual, since it can represent any cup. Though "the CUP" implies a particular individual, it requires some further mechanism to tie the representation to a particular contextual cup.

Typically, the way infants are tested is by introducing one or two individual objects into the here-and-now context and then asking the infant to track this individual and that individual as they undergo an occlusion. The type of occlusion typically used will produce a perceptual masking and banish the object related sensory and iconic memory codes. Following this, the infant is asked to make individuation or identity judgements when this and/or that individual appears once more.We therefore owe an account, not only of how objects come to be represented as belonging to kinds, but also of how particular individuals can be tracked and referred to by the cognitive system.

Object Index

A key construct in theoretical framework for object tracking by infants is the object index. We hypothesize that when one attends to an object, the brain assigns a mental "pointer" or index to that object. The index "sticks" to, and thus tracks, the object as it moves, even if it moves behind an occluder. The sticky index allows the infant to continue to attend to the object while occluded, though, inevitably, this demands working memory resources. The construct of an object index is drawn from studies of adult attention and, specifically, as already noted, has much in common with the idea of an "object file".

We hypothesize that an index forms the core of the object representation that an infant constructs in working memory while attending to a physical object. One analogy to the notion of an object index is a mental finger that points at an object in the world. Although a pointing finger contains no information about the object at which it points, it allows rapid access to the object, without an exhaustive search. Straining the analogy somewhat, a note containing descriptive information about the object pointed at (e.g., color, shape, or size) might optionally be glued to the pointing finger.

Another-perhaps more useful-analogy can be drawn between the nonverbal index and demonstrative words in language. A bare index might be thought of as analogous to indicating an object by uttering, "THAT!"

Two objects might be indicated by "THIS!" and "THAT!" Descriptive information might optionally be added: "THIS is RED!" and "THAT is GREEN!" An object index constructed in working memory can serve to interface bottomup sensory information with information stored in long-term memory, e.g., object kind information. As we saw, a representation of object kind, e.g., CUP, cannot by itself be used as the representation of a particular individual object because kind representations are generic. However, this long-term representation might be combined under appropriate circumstances with an object index to yield the working memory representation, "THIS is a CUP." Since the sticky index, THIS, will continuously point to a particular object through changes of location, it allows the infant to track a particular cup throughout an episode.

There are obvious reasons for assuming that working memory plays a key role in the on-line tracking of small sets of objects through occlusion. Information about the objects needs to be maintained through the period of occlusion. The effect of occlusion is not simply the absence of sensory input from the occluded objects, but also that sensory input from unrelated surfaces and objects continues to be processed and overwrites the older information in the sensory system. There are therefore severe spatiotemporal constraints on what information about occluded objects the visual system can maintain on its own, without the assistance of attention and working memory. Information gleaned from attending to an object and to its behavior throughout an episode will often find its way into long-term memory. This means that object indexing in working memory will be an important conduit for information in the process of learning about object kinds.

Working memory appears to comprise a set of behaviorally and neurally specialized components in prefrontal cortex. Among those commonly recognized are verbal, visual, spatial, and object short-term stores plus an executive control component. It has been known for almost 2 decades that the lateral prefrontal cortex has a central role in working memory functions. Recent neurophysiological and imaging studies have revealed several distinct subsystems within this area. Some researchers assume that the subsystems reflect a functional division of labor, that there are separate circuits for the maintenance of memory codes and for the manipulation of memory codes. Others have found evidence for a complex stimulusdependent segregation: first, between verbal and visual working memory and more recently within the visual domain; working memory for objects appears to be mediated by more ventral frontal regions, while spatial working memory is mediated by more dorsal frontal regions. Object-and space-based systems of the frontal lobe are presumed to correspond to the functional segregation of earlier processing stages, such as the ventral (object discrimination or "what") and the dorsal (spatial localization or "where") visual pathways. A general feature of working, as opposed to long-term, memory is that it is capacity limited.

Capacity limitations in visual working memory have not been so extensively studied as those in verbal working memory. However, early work suggested that visual working memory capacity is severely limited. Cells in the dorsolateral prefrontal cortex receive inputs from the parietal dorsal visual system ("where"), while cells in the ventrolateral prefrontal cortex receive inputs from the inferotemporal ventral visual system ("what"). Neurons with delay activity in lateral prefrontal cortex that were selective for either object location or for object feature information. Interestingly, around half the neurons with delay activity showed tuning to both location and feature information, suggesting that the prefrontal working memory systems are an important site for integrating such information. It is likely, then, that these systems play an important role in the binding of features to the object representation.

There is also behavioral evidence that the prefrontal cortex undergoes major maturational changes during the second half of the first year, a finding which is also supported by anatomical data.We hypothesize then that the maturation of these frontal, integrating, working memory systems plays an important role in the increasingly robust individuation and identification abilities infants display toward the end of the 1st year.

The current literature contains disputes and discrepant findings surrounding the age at which infants can individuate objects by feature. While it may take some considerable time to resolve these questions, we want to argue that there is considerably more theoretical space that is usually assumed. We should pay more attention to the question of mechanism and cognitive architecture and be more mindful of performance systems as well as of competence and representational systems. There are many properties that over the past 20 years or so infants have been shown to represent, properties such as solidity, causal role, rigidity, compressibility, shape, color, and so forth. But showing that such properties are representable is not the same thing as showing under what circumstances such property representations find their way into particular object working memory representations. Nor have we measured the limits on infant object working memory, the role of attention in processing different object properties, or the limits on parallel individuation and identity judgements. Until we do, we shall be missing an important part of the story of how infants pick up information from the world and acquire long-term object kind representations.

Slant Perception

Since stimulus information available to an observer remains constant over age, developmental changes in perceptual ability must reflect age related changes in information utilization. Few attempts have been made, however, to assess the developmental changes in information utilization, perhaps because of the difficulty in specifying the information necessary for a particular task. This difficulty has been overcome in the area of space perception and specifically the perception of slant. The informational basis for slant perception has been discussed by Purdy, Flock, and Rosinski. Purdy, in a mathematical analysis, has demonstrated that for static, monocular arrays the relative rate of change of certain texture parameters (namely, the height, width, area, and spacing of elements) defines a texture gradient which potentially specifies surface slant. It has been shown that there is an invariant relationship between the information provided by a texture gradient and physical slant. The gradient available at any point on the surface is directly related to the cotangent of the angle formed by the surface and the line of regard. Consequently, the gradients unambiguously specify absolute slant of the surface relative to any arbitrary reference axis.

There are two possible ways in which developmental

improvements in information utilization may occur, given such an invariant relationship between texture gradient and physical slant. An individual's ability to differentiate a gradient may improve; that is, his ability to compare texture elements and extract the relative rate of change which defines a gradient may improve with age. As the ability to differentiate a gradient improves, perceptual judgment should improve.

Gibson argued that improvements in differentiation (i.e., in extracting information from stimulation) accompany perceptual development. However, improvement in differentiation is not sufficient to account for perceptual development. One must also pick up the relationship between these visual inputs and those of other perceptual systems and detect the multimodal invariant relationship among these sources of information. This extraction of invariant relationships is a crucial aspect of development, since potential information may not be effective if it is not related to physical layout: A particular gradient may provide no information (may be meaningless) unless the relationship between that optical gradient and physical slant is established.

In studying the effectiveness of various texture gradients, they presented stimulus displays which provided either linear perspective gradient information or compression (foreshortening) gradient information. One must, in order to extract a linear perspective gradient, compare the relative width of texture elements along successive portions of the display. Although the minimal processing capabilities (estimation and comparison of angular extents) necessary for the differentiation of the two gradients are the same, differences in effectiveness were found. Perspective gradients provided a more effective basis for slant judgment than did compression gradients. These results suggest that the differential effectiveness of the two gradients may be due to differences in the degree to which each gradient had been associated with the physical slant it specified.

Although Purdy's analysis of texture gradient information assumed that each texture element had the same physical size, both Purdy and Flock have shown that this analysis applies to irregularly textured surfaces. If the size of texture elements varies over the surface, the gradient is defined as the rate of change in the average size of an element. That is, the gradient is the relative rate of change of the average size of a texture element across the display. This extension of texture gradient theory to irregular surfaces has important implications. Since size averaging must be used, the differentiation of a gradient should be more difficult from irregular surfaces than from regular ones. However, since the gradient projected from regularly or irregularly textured surfaces both define a particular slant, judgments should, in principle, be equally accurate once the gradient has been differentiated. If perceptual improvement is the result of improved gradient extraction, children should have considerably more trouble than adults in judging the slant of irregularly textured surfaces. Children's performance with regular textures may be nearly as accurate as that of adults. Regularity of texture element size had no significant effect on the accuracy of slant judgments. These data suggest that adults are able to use texture gradients specifying slant in spite of size variability; that is, they are able to overcome the increased difficulty of differentiating the gradient.

5

Influence of Media on Mental Growth

As boys pass from childhood to manhood, they develop their moral and ethical code. They learn to handle emerging sexuality. They clarify conceptions of gender roles. And they prepare for their future careers. While young people have traditionally been guided in these paths by familiar sources-family, friends, religion-today's boys are increasingly influenced by an ever-expanding and pervasive media.

From an early age, boys are especially active users of media, watching hours of television, movies, music videos, and sports, listening to radio and CDs, surfing the Internet, and playing computer and video games. Researchers have suggested that the cumulative impact of these media may make them some of the most influential forces in their lives, especially during adolescence.

Yet there is remarkably little research on media's influence on boys. To explore this important issue and to expand on previous research on gender, Children Now commissioned research into the media's messages about masculinity and their impact on boys. In-depth content studies analyzed messages in the primetime television shows, movies, and music videos most frequently watched by boys. Included in the research is a national poll of 1,200 young people (ages 10 to 17) and focus groups in which boys offered their own insights into the media they consume. We learned that, in spite of the complex and changing work and family experiences of real-life men, media portrayals do not reflect this complexity. Rather, messages and images remain strongly stereotypical. Indeed, men are pictured in a variety of roles. Yet across all characterizations, those who are admired share predictable and timeworn attributes.

Men are expected to be leaders. Whether exhibiting positive or negative behaviour, they must be confident, successful, funny, and athletic. They are characteristically violent and angry and, regardless of circumstances, they are not to cry. Men are also seen as problem-solvers, though the problems men face and the solutions they use vary depending upon the man's race. And finally, men in the media are defined not by their relationships (as are women) but by their careers.

Today's young people, while consuming unprecedented quantities of media, experience a contradiction between their own reality and media messages about masculinity. While they identify the characteristics and behaviours so familiarly attributed to men, they also recognize that the men and boys they see on TV are not like themselves nor the boys and men in their own lives.

Gender roles are shifting. Media influence is growing. And the next generation is defining its place in the adult world. How young people absorb and integrate the media's images along with their personal experiences will have a profound impact on the expectations and behaviour of a new generation of men.

Children between the ages of 10 and 17 most often spend their time watching television programs, listening to music on CDs and tapes, and listening to the radio. Television is the top medium of daily use for all children through the eighth grade, when music and radio then surpass television. After watching television and listening to music, kids enjoy playing computer or video games, watching movies on a VCR, or reading magazines. Children are least likely to read a newspaper or go to the movies on a daily basis.

Music videos, comedies, and cartoons are the television programs kids most frequently watch. After these types of programming, kids enjoy sports programmes and talk shows like Jerry Springer and Oprah.

Boys are more likely than girls to watch television, play video games, and use the Internet. Although both boys and girls are most likely to watch television programs almost daily, a larger percentage of boys do so than girls (81% vs. 75%). Boys are more than twice as likely as girls to play video games (40% vs. 18%) and are also more likely to use the Internet (15% vs. 10%). Girls are slightly more likely to read magazines and more likely to listen to CDs and tapes on a regular basis.

Boys' favourite television programs and movies are comedies and are most likely to be ones that recommend parental guidance. Over half of the television programs and movies that boys (ages 12-17) watch are comedies. The television programs that boys watch most frequently are rated TV-PG and the movies they watch are most likely to be rated PG-13.

Boys are more likely to watch sports and cartoons and girls are more likely to watch talk shows. Boys are five times more likely than girls to watch sports programming on a regular basis (33% vs. 7%) and enjoy cartoons daily (36% vs. 27%). Girls are more than twice as likely to watch talk shows (25% girls vs. 10% boys).

Boys choose boys, girls choose both. When asked to choose 3 television role models, 80% of boys choose male personalities, while only 16% choose a female. Conversely, 57% of girls choose males and 59% choose females. Further, 43% of boys choose only males, while only 25% of girls choose only females.

Boys say humour, girls say appearance. Boys are much more likely than girls to list "funny" as their top reason for choosing an individual to be one of their favourites (56% vs. 38%), whereas girls are almost three times as likely to say "because they are pretty or handsome" (29% vs. 11%).

Media and Sex

Sexual activity is shown in almost half of the sample of media most popular with boys. Movies in the sample portray the most sexual activity, with over two thirds containing some level of sexual content (67%). Of those movies, over half of the depictions are coded as serious in nature (60%). Almost half of television shows (48%) depict sexual activity, half of which are significant to the plot. The sexual content in 58% of these shows is light and comic in nature.

A majority of children say that men and boys on

television are often portrayed as focused on the opposite sex. Most children say men and boys often are shown talking about the opposite sex (75%), wanting to have a girlfriend (74%), and wanting to kiss or have sex (69%).

Media and Violence

Some violence appears in over half of the sample of television shows and movies most popular with boys. Across media in sample, movies contain the most violence. All of the movies in the sample contain violent depictions, with frequent violence in 60% of those viewed. Further, the violence tends to be serious in nature and in nearly 90% of the cases, the violence is significant to the plot or a major feature of the film. Television shows have much less violence than movies, with almost two thirds of shows (64%) in our sample having no violence at all. Of the television shows that contain violence, more than half of the depictions are light or comic (56%) or incidental to the plot (56%).

Accordingly, children say they see violence most often in movies and video games. Almost two thirds of children say they see violence in movies a lot of the time (62%). Similarly, when asked what they thought was the most violent medium, a plurality of children say movies (49%) and more than one fourth say video games (27%). Further, 82% of children say they see violence in video games "a lot" or "some of the time."

Almost three fourths of children describe males on television as violent. Children say that the adjective "violent" describes males on television well (72%). There is little difference in boys' and girls' perceptions. However, boys who name a cartoon character as their favourite television character are more likely to view television males as violent than boys who choose a male or female character.

More than two thirds of children describe men and boys on television as angry. When asked how well the adjective angry describes males on television, 69% of children say it describes them well. Older boys are most likely to view television males as angry, with more than one fourth of 16-17 year-olds (27%) noting that the adjective describes males "very well." Asian Pacific American children are least likely to think that angry describes males on television "very well" (16%).

Influence of Characters

Children see men on TV as leaders and problem-solvers. More than three fourths of children describe boys and men on television as being leaders often (78%) and almost three fourths describe them as solving problems often (73%). Boys are more likely than girls to say that television males are shown as leaders and problem-solvers. Further, a plurality of children believe in charge (44%), courageous (43%), and intelligent (40%) can be used to describe a majority of boys and men on television very well. These perceptions correspond with the actual portrayals of male characters on television. Almost all of the male characters in the sample engage in problem solving behaviours (94%) and almost half are leaders or demonstrate initiative (40%).

Children believe that television males are funny. Overwhelmingly, children say that boys and men on television are well-described as funny (98%). Kids hold this perception across racial, gender, and age lines-

majorities of all groups of young people believe that a sense of humour describes the males on TV. Children also think that television males acted dumb often (72%). While this characteristic might be considered a sign of immaturity, it may also be a trait associated with being funny. Acting dumb can be laughable, but positive. Notably, younger and older boys assert that their positive role models need to have a sense of humour.

Men on television appear confident, successful, and athletic. Ninety-one percent of children polled believe that men on television are usually portrayed as confident, and 94% are likely to use the term successful to describe men on television. Children also believe that TV males are athletic (90%) and say that they often see males on television playing sports (80%). Accordingly, a majority of children contend that weak is not an appropriate description of boys and men on entertainment television (58% believe weak does not describe males on TV well). However, heavy media users are more inclined to say that they sometimes see weak male characters. Thirty-five percent of boys with heavy media use and 42% of girls with heavy media use say that weak describes male characters "somewhat well."

Across boys' favourite media, men are more closely identified with the working world and high prestige positions, while women are identified more often with their domestic status. Male characters are more often shown at their place of work, while female characters are more frequently shown at home. Eighty-eight percent of children polled say that they see males on television in the working world, and over one third say that they never see television males performing domestic chores such as cooking or cleaning. Correspondingly, relationship status is more obvious for female characters and occupational status is more obvious for males. While approximately one third of female characters are married or involved in a serious romantic relationship, marital status is unidentifiable for nearly half of the male characters. Likewise, occupational status is unknown for nearly half of the female characters. When her status can be determined, the female character is more likely to be shown in traditionally female occupations such as teacher, student, homemaker, or clerical worker. Male characters are more likely to be shown in higher status occupations, such as executive/CEO, professional, or business owner, and are also more frequently cast in traditionally male-dominated fields like politics, the military, and law enforcement.

Television, movies, and music videos most popular with boys present a world of males, especially straight White males. Overall, males constitute just over two thirds of the population represented in these media (68%) and two-thirds of them are White. This imbalance is most pronounced in movies where there is only one female character to every three males. Male and female characters are almost entirely heterosexual, with only 1% portrayed as homosexual or bisexual.

Although male characters in the media display a range of emotional behaviour, including fear, anger, grief, and pain, they seldom cry. While more than four in ten male characters (43%) express some sort of emotional behaviour, very few expressions involve crying.

Children believe that men and boys are least likely to be seen crying or showing vulnerability on television. Overwhelmingly, children in the national poll say that they rarely see men or boys showing signs of vulnerability, such as crying, on television (57% every now and then, 18% never). Among certain populations, the perception that men on TV never cry is particularly strong-24% of Latino boys and 22% of Asian Pacific American boys say that they have never seen men or boys on television shedding a tear. Among boys who choose male television characters as their favourites, 23% say that men never cry on TV.

Further, kids in the focus groups say that television rarely portrays men expressing their feelings, crying, or showing anything that might be considered vulnerability. Thirty-eight percent of boys and 24% of girls polled believe that sensitive is an inaccurate description of television boys and men. Likewise, 40% of boys and 36% of girls in the poll think that the adjective emotionalis also inappropriate.

Emotional behaviour by male characters is equally likely to be reinforced positively and negatively. Because most male displays of emotion are done in isolation (44%), there is frequently no response from other characters. However, the displays that involve other characters are equally likely to be reinforced positively (24%) as negatively (26%). Often, characters have several dilemmas and motivations in a storyline, falling into primary and secondary categories. Looking at the males on the TV shows and in the movies that boys watch most, there are several interesting patterns regarding their characters' problems, motivations, and solutions.

Work is the greatest source of problems and motivation for male characters, especially for White men. More than four in ten male characters have primary problems and more than one in five male characters have secondary problems involving their work. However, while almost half of the White males have primary problems at work, less than one third of the men of colour do. Problems and motivations differ between minority and White male characters.

Minority male characters are more likely than White male characters to have primary problems involving family, personal, romantic, or friendship issues. Romantic relationships provide the most primary problems for minority men (30%), followed by work (29%), family (23%), friendship (17%), and personal issues (16%). The corresponding figures for White male characters (aside from work at 48%) are consistently lower: family (16%), romance (12%), friendship (11%), and personal issues (15%).

White male characters are consistently more motivated than minorities by succeeding in work (25% primary, 22% secondary), preventing and managing disaster (7% primary, 8% secondary), and pleasing non-romantic others (2% primary, 6% secondary). Yet they are also far more motivated by being antisocial (8% primary and 15% secondary vs. 1% primary and 4% secondary for minorities).

Minority male characters are consistently more motivated than Whites (primarily and secondarily) by pro-social behaviour/helping others (29% primary, 40% secondary), but also by making money (6% primary and 18% secondary vs. 3% primary and 7% secondary for Whites) and having sex (6% primary and 6% secondary vs. 1% primary and 5% secondary for Whites).

Problems facing and motivations driving male characters correlate to the age of the character: Older adults (43%) and settled adults (53%) are most likely to experience work related problems, while adolescents experience the most friendship and romance problems (46% and 42% respectively). The largest age group in the sample-young adults-experience primary problems related to work (38%), romance (25%), and personal areas (22%) most frequently. Correspondingly, adult males are most frequently motivated by succeeding in work (35%), as are young adults (19%). Adolescent characters are equally motivated by pleasing a romantic partner (33%) and pro-social behaviour/helping others (33%). Young adults are also highly motivated by pleasing a romantic partner (17%).

Male characters demonstrate initiative or leadership ability most often as their way of solving problems. Almost half of the male characters in our sample (45%) show initiative or leadership ability as a means to solve the problem at hand. White males are more likely than minority males (49% vs. 40%) to demonstrate this type of problem-solving behaviour.

Almost one third of male characters offer advice/ support or talk about their feelings as a way of solving problems. In sample, 29% of male characters provide advice and support or discuss their emotions to deal with an issue or resolve a situation. Men of colour are more likely than White men to offer advice and support as a problem-solving strategy (38% vs. 26%).

One in five male characters employs some form of physical aggression (21% with weapons, 19% without weapons) to solve problems. Men of colour are more likely than White men to engage in physical aggression with weapons (27% vs. 19%). White men are more likely than men of colour to engage in physical aggression without weapons (21% vs. 15%).

Male characters employ pro-social behaviours about

as often as antisocial behaviours to solve problems. In sample, male characters use pro-social and antisocial means with nearly equal frequency to solve their problems. Almost half of the male characters in the sample use a combination of both types of behaviours. Almost two thirds of the characters (66%) use at least one type of pro-social behaviour (such as taking initiative/ leadership, offering advice or talking about feelings, asking for advice, helping others, providing affection, delivering praise) when solving their problems. Men of colour are more likely than White men to demonstrate pro-social problem-solving behaviours (71% vs. 64%). Similarly, two thirds of the characters (67%) use antisocial behaviours (aggression with and without weapons, deception/lying, dominance, noncompliance/ defiance, verbal aggression, ridiculing/insulting, lawbreaking, arguing, ignoring, dismissing) to solve their problems. White men are more likely than men of colour to exhibit antisocial problem-solving behaviours (71% vs. 57%).

Minority characters are more likely to use sexual behaviours to solve their problems, while White characters are more likely to use deception, dominance, and ridicule. Although only a very small proportion of characters employ sexual behaviours in problem solving (7%), people of colour were nine times more likely than Whites to be shown using these strategies (18% vs. 2%). Sexual behaviours include: talking about sex, sexual talk in and outside a relationship, and sexual activity in and outside a relationship. White male characters are more likely than minority male characters to use deception (23% vs. 15%), dominance (20% vs. 12%), and ridicule (10% vs. 3%) to solve problems.

When dealing with their problems, young adult male characters use the most antisocial behaviours and adolescents use the most sexual behaviours. Almost three fourths of young adult male characters (73%) use antisocial behaviours to solve problems, which is higher than any other age group. Further, more than one in five adolescent male characters (22%) is shown using sexual behaviours to solve his problems, compared to 7% for all male characters.

Across race and gender, the majority of children believe that the boys and men they see on television are different from themselves, the boys they know, their fathers, and other adult male relatives.

More than half of boys (58%) say the male figures they see on television are different from themselves or other adult male relatives; only one third of boys (34%) say the males they see on television are like themselves or other adult male relatives.

Latino and Asian Pacific American boys cite in disproportionate numbers (67% and 63% respectively) the differences between themselves and other males they see on TV, while African American boys are slightly more supportive of the notion that the males they see on television are accurate to their lives (37% vs. 34% of all boys). Notably, two thirds of younger boys (ages 10-12) say TV does not offer a realistic picture of themselves and their male relatives, as compared to 54% of older boys (ages 13-17). More than half of girls (58%) believe that the males they see on television are different from the males they know in real life; less than one third (31%) believe that they are similar.

Minority girls are more likely than White girls to believe the portrayals of males are different from males in their own lives. High numbers of African American, Asian Pacific American, and Latina girls say the portrayal on television is different from males they know (71%, 70% and 68% respectively), compared to 53% of White girls.

While the majority of children believe television males are different from those in real life, they give varying reasons for the difference. Fifty-eight percent of children say that boys and men on television are different from those they know personally. Children offer many reasons for the difference including "they behave differently" (27%), "they look different" (14%), and "they don't have real problems" (10%). Across race, the top two responses are "they behave differently" or "they look different," with African American children the most likely to say "they behave differently than me" (32%). Interestingly, boys are slightly more likely than girls to cite behavioral differences (29% vs. 26%), whereas girls are slightly more likely to cite appearance (18% vs. 10%) and not having real problems (13% vs. 8%).

Portrayals of success on television are not necessarily aligned with young people's ideas of real-life success. Compare one boy's personal ideas of success, "When they are older, if they have a job and if they have a good family and stuff—that is successful, "with other boys' perceptions of success on TV, "A rich guy with a lot of good clothes and a huge house and everything. . . and a beautiful wife. "Thirty-eight percent of the children polled think that "having money" indicates success on entertainment television, but only 21% think that it is a realistic indicator of success. Thus, many kids believe that financial wealth is an over-represented sign of success on television, stronger than it is in real life. Correspondingly, children also believe that some of their ideas of real-life success are under represented on television. For example, 24% of children believe that having a good job/career is real-life success but only 16% believe that it is depicted as such on television. Another 21% of children believe having the respect of family and friends is a realistic indicator of success, but only 10% find that it is portrayed as such by entertainment television.

Moreover, some kids criticize television portrayals of success because of their racial implications. Today's boys navigate a perilous path toward manhood. Even if he is raised in a healthy, loving environment, a boy must sort out powerful societal messages that limit and restrict the definition of masculinity-the definition of who he should become. And he will hear and see these messages reinforced and amplified on television, in the movies, in music videos, and in video games-throughout his favourite sources of entertainment. Serious or subtle, the media's role in defining manhood is significant.

Influence of Sports Programmmes

Sports programming plays a significant role in the media messages that American boys receive today. Around 98% of U.S. boys ages 8 to 17 consume some form of sports-related media, 82% do so at least a couple of times a week, and 90% watch televised sports. While a full range of American boys watch sports, the effects of their media consumption may differ depending on who they are and what messages are being sent. By looking at the quality of a representative selection of sports programmes and their accompanying commercials, Children Now begins to explore the many messages that sports programming-athletes, games, broadcast networks, commentators, promoters, commercials presents to its audience.

Boys are five times more likely than girls to watch sports programmes on a regular basis. On average, one out of three boys across all races watch every day. With its fundamentally male "cast"—athletes and anchors, coaches and commentators—sports programming sends uniquely powerful messages about masculine behaviour.

Aggression and violence among men is depicted as exciting and rewarding behaviour. One of sports coverage's dominant messages is that the most aggressive athletes are rewarded. Viewers are continually immersed in images that highlight and commentary that praises athletes who most successfully employ physical, aggressive play, as well as toughness. This message was found most often in NBA games, comprising 40 of the 66 examples from sample. During the NFL games, there were 15 examples of this message, as commentators enthusiastically described and replayed scenes of players who got "buried," "stuffed," or "walloped" by the defense, or "cleaned out" or "wiped" by the blocker. There also were several instances of this theme during Extreme Sports (4 times), Major League Baseball games (4 times), and Sports Center (3 times).

Sports coverage emphasizes the notion that violence is to be expected. Fights, near-fights, threats of fights or other violent actions are found in sports coverage and often verbally framed in sarcastic language that suggests that this kind of action is acceptable. This message was found most frequently on Sports Center (10 times), followed by the NFL games (7 times), Major League Baseball games (2 times), NBA games (2 times), and Extreme Sports (1 time). And in an NFL game, a broadcaster described a brief scuffle between players, explaining that they were simply "making their acquaintance."

Athletes who are "playing with pain" or "giving up their body for the team" are often portrayed as heroes. Commentators laud athletes who engage in dangerous plays or compete while injured; conversely, they sometimes criticize athletes who remove themselves from games due to injuries, often raising questions about their manhood. This "playing with pain" theme was most common in the NFL games (15 instances), followed by Extreme Sports (12 instances), SportsCenter (9 instances), and NBA games (6 instances). Sports commentators continually depict and replay incidents of athletes taking big hits and engaging in reckless acts of speed and violent crashes. Showing guts in the face of danger and disaster is a common theme among sports programs and is especially prominent in Extreme Sports, appearing 21 different times during the sample week.

Games are often promoted by creating or inflating conflict between two star athletes. Sports announcers often frame team games as individual one-on-one contests between two well-known individual players. This theme was particularly prominent in the NBA games, with 29 instances.

White males dominate the world of sports commentary. The voices of authority on the sports shows surveyed are almost exclusively those of White males. More than three-fourths of sports announcers in the sample are White males (77%) who conduct the "play-by-play," ongoing "colour commentary" in the NFL, NBA, and Major League Baseball games, as well as on SportsCenter, in Wrestling, and in Extreme Sports. Women and people of colour are presented sparingly and, with the exception of ESPN's use of a woman and an African American male co-anchor, play minor supporting roles. In this sample, they rarely appear as the main voices of authority-"in the booth," conducting "play-by-play" or providing ongoing "color commentary." White females and African American males each account for only 10% of sports commentators; African American females account for only 3% of announcers. Further, there were no Latino or Asian Pacific American sports commentators in sample of sports shows. While there were few overtly racist images or comments, sports programs occasionally reinforced racial stereotypes or called attention to race/ethnicity in commentary.

Racial stereotypes or comments were found during the NBA and NFL games (7 and 6 instances, respectively), followed by SportsCenter (3 instances), Wrestling (3 instances), and Extreme Sports (1 instance). Further, SportsCenter commentators have lauded African American athletes for their "natural athleticism." Women athletes receive very little coverage on sports programs that supposedly feature both men and women athletes.

Surprisingly, ESPN's SportsCenter shows in sample devote a mere 3% of news time to women's sports. Even Extreme Sports programming that is seen as an "alternative" open to men and women devotes only 1% of its coverage to women athletes. Women are largely absent from the sports programs that boys watch and when they do appear, they are portrayed in stereotypical ways. The lack of women in male-dominated sports programs gives their rare appearances greater significance. For the most part, women appear in sports programs as sex objects, supportive spouses, or spectators on the sidelines, cheering the men on.

The incidence of women being used as sex objects or props was most common in Wrestling (13 times), followed by Extreme Sports (5 times), NFL games (4 times), and the NBA (3 times). In Wrestling the shows utilized scantily clad women to escort the male wrestlers to the ring, often with announcers discussing their "feminine virtues." In the NBA and NFL games, cameras cut to close-up shots of the cheerleaders, often focusing on their breasts.

Sports programming reveals a powerful commercial alliance between celebrity athletes, corporations, and the broadcasting network. NBA stats and player profiles during game commentary are usually "brought to you by" a named corporate sponsor. Further, brand name manufacturers of equipment used in the games are often highlighted by commercials during the event and by broadcast logos shown in opening program shots.

Commercial sponsorships and tie-ins: While some male athletes of color do play prominent roles in sports programming, people of color in general are under represented in the sports programming commercials that boys watch and appear primarily in stereotypical and/ or background roles. Over half of all the commercials recorded feature only White people (52.2%). Removing from the pool commercials that do not show any people at all (91 commercials), the proportion of White-only advertisements rises to 59.7%. People of color almost never appear in commercials unless the commercial also has White people in it ("multi-racial" commercials). Out of 722 commercials, only 28 feature African Americans by themselves, only 3 feature Latinos by themselves (all on NFL programming), and only 2 feature Asian Pacific Americans by themselves.

While "multi-racial" commercials may constitute a significant proportion of a program's advertising (32.7% of NBA, 32% of Wrestling), people of color are often relegated to minor roles, literally in the "background" of scenes that feature White people. In the background, an African American man walks by quickly. In sports programming that boys consume, the relative invisibility of women magnifies the importance of the female images that do appear. Although women are more visible in the commercials than in the programs themselves, the frequency and quality of representation raises concerns. Women rarely appear without men in the sports programming commercials in the sample. While 44.2% of the commercials with people feature only men, 4.4% feature only women. Nearly every one of the 91 commercials that portray no people has a male voice-over. Including these commercials pushes the percentage of male-only advertisements to over 50%.

Many sports programming commercials that boys watch play on male insecurities about being "man" enough. A common formula in commercials is to play on the insecurities of the audience, convincing them that purchasing a particular product will help them overcome their fears, embarrassments, and shortcomings. In sports programming, many of the commercials play on male fears of being a geek or a nerd who is not cool, aggressive, or attractive to women. Commercials for products such as Rogaine (hair loss) feature formerly insecure, unattractive men who acquire confidence and success after using the product.

Traditionally masculine images of speed, danger, and aggression are often used in the sports programming commercials that boys watch. Echoing the images that pervade sports programming, commercials often employ storylines that emphasize speed, danger, or aggressive behaviour to attract viewers to their products. Around 27% of the commercials on Extreme Sports place actors in such situations. Women often appear in stereotypical and/or background roles.

The images of women as sexual objects, prizes, and supportive props for men's success in sports programming are reinforced by the commercials that play during the games. On average, a sports programming viewer watching shows and commercials will see these images twice an hour.

In commercials that feature both women and men, women are often cast as beautiful and sexual rewards for men who purchase the right product. A typical storyline involves the transformation of a formerly nerdy or insecure man who is now adored and desired by beautiful women. Accordingly, some women are also cast as "controlling," "emotional" wives and girl friends who must be rejected in favour of beautiful, sexy women. In a Sony PlayStation spot shown on Extreme Sports and during NBA games, a male is shown with a female watching a romantic film. The male is then ridiculed and taunted by cartoon characters for being "whipped," watching a "chick flick," and doomed to domestic chores. At the end of the commercial, the female is harassed by a cartoon clown and locked out of the room, while the male is playing a video game and accompanied by a big-breasted cartoon woman.

Ninety percent of boys regularly or often watch televised sports programs, with their accompanying commercial advertisements. According to the sports programming that boys consume most, a real man is strong, tough, aggressive, and above all, a winner in what is still a man's world. To be a winner, he must be willing to compromise his own long-term health by showing guts in the face of danger, by fighting other men when necessary, and by "playing hurt" when he's injured. He must avoid being soft; he must be the aggressor, both on the "battlefields" of sports and in his consumption choices. Whether he is playing sports or making choices about which products to purchase, his aggressiveness will win him the ultimate prize: the adoring attention of beautiful women and the admiration of other men.

Child Pornography

Most of us would agree that child pornography constitutes sexualised pictures involving children. However what precisely is meant by sexualised can vary depending on whether a legal or the more subjective perspective of the adult with a sexual interest in children is taken. Legal definitions tend to emphasize obscene or sexual content as an essential quality of the images, but of course such definitions may vary depending on the legislature within a given country. This is a particular problem in relation to the Internet where cultural, moral and legal variations make it difficult to define "pornographic" in such a global society.

The International Criminal Police Organization (Interpol) standing working group on offences against minors defines Child pornography as: "...the consequence of the exploitation or sexual abuse perpetrated against a child. It can be defined as any means of depicting or promoting sexual abuse of a child, including print and/or audio, centred on sex acts or the genital organs of children." A similar emphasis on the sexual nature of the material can be found in the u.k.'s Criminal Justice Protection of Children Act of 1978 which was amended in 1994 to state that, "it is an offence for a person:

a) to take, or permit to be taken or to make, any indecent photographs or pseudophotographs of a child;

b) to distribute or show such indecent photographs or pseudo- photographs."

However, while such definitions are clearly important from a legislative perspective, they are of limited value in helping us understand why such images are produced or collected, or the function that they might have in offending behaviour. Over emphasis on highly sexualised or obscene images deflects from the fact that any image can be sexualised and fantasized over, and what makes that image of the child important to the adult is the psychological role it plays in arousal and masturbation.

Legal definitions enable us to draw boundaries, but do not help in delineating the problem. Indeed, it may be argued that such definitions give rise to the notion of "good" and "bad" offenders, depending on the degree to which the viewer finds the material objectionable. Collections of child pornography do not arise by accident, but by the deliberate choices an individual makes to acquire material. Nor are such pictures a homogeneous category.

By emphasizing a psychological approach to such images, we can identify a range of discernibly different pictures that are collected by adults with a sexual interest in children, only some of which may be illegal. It is possible to construct a continuum of increased deliberate sexual victimization, ranging from everyday and perhaps accidental pictures involving either no overt erotic content, or minimal content (such as the depiction of a child in their underwear) to pictures showing actual rape and penetration of a child, or other gross acts of obscenity. Such a continuum may be helpful in characterizing the nature of a given collection, and may also elucidate factors that may enable and sustain offender behaviour. Central to this is an acknowledgement that child pornography is not a victimless crime. Regardless of the content of the picture, each time that an image of a child is accessed for a sexual purpose, it victimizes the individual concerned.

A descriptive analysis identified 10 levels of severity, based on increasing sexual victimization, and quite deliberately included pictures that do not fall within any legal definition of child pornography. These 10 levels of severity can be briefly described as follows:

— Level 1: Indicative (non-erotic/sexualised pictures)

— Level 2: Nudist (naked or semi-naked in legitimate settings/sources)

— Level 3: Erotica (surreptitious photographs showing underwear/nakedness)

— Level 4: Posing (deliberate posing suggesting sexual content)

— Level 5: Erotic Posing (deliberate sexual or provocative poses)

— Level 6: Explicit Erotic Posing (emphasis on genital areas)

— Level 7: Explicit Sexual Activity (explicit activity, but not involving an adult)

— Level 8: Assault (sexual assault involving adult)

— Level 9: Gross Assault (penetrative assault involving adult)

— Level 10: Sadistic/Bestiality (sexual images involving pain or animal)

It is important to emphasize in relation to collections of pictures, that even Level 1 images can be sexualised and fantasized over, and may be used to both promote and sustain sexual fantasy. It is also the case that boundaries between pictures can be blurred, but such a typology encompasses the wide array of material attractive to the adult with a sexual interest in children, and places the emphasis back on the child as victim, rather than the end-product of the obscene photograph. This is of particular importance in the context of Level 3 pictures (pictures which are secretly or surreptitiously taken). Lack of knowledge of victimization by the subject does not diminish its gravity.

Collections of pictures are rarely a random aggregation of individual images. Most pictures occur as part of a series and it is usual for such series to have a narrative or thematic link. The narrative may be an aid to fantasy and filling gaps in the series may be highly reinforcing to the collector. Locating a picture, or a series of pictures, at some level on the continuum needs to be considered in the context of other issues relating to a collection. These include the size of the collection and the obsessional qualities relating to its organization, and storage, the principle themes illustrated, the presence of new or private material, and the age of the children depicted in the pictures. Recent evidence suggests that the age of children in new pornography is reducing with the implication that such victims may be less able to disclose the abuse than would older children. Its principal practical value (as distinct from its research role) has been to facilitate the identification of new children involved in child pornography, as distinct from existing material.

The Copine Project was one of the famous study which addressed children's vulnerability in relation to the new technologies, and in particular issues related to child pornography and the Internet. An important feature of the project, which has been funded by grants both from private sources, has been its links with the law enforcement community in Ireland, the United Kingdom, Belgium, the Netherlands and the United States. Currently the Project is involved in three research areas: the maintenance of a reference data base of child pornography; an assessment of dangerousness in paedophiles through their collection of child pornography; the nature and incidence of child sex tourism and child trafficking in Europe. A new project concerned with victim identification will begin shortly.

Through the database, the Project has extensive records of the nicknames and Network News Transport Protocols (nntp) posting host addresses under which newsgroup postings have been made. In total, the database includes approximately 80,000 still pictures and 400+ video clips. Of the 80,000 images, more than half are of girls. Of those pictures of girls categorised as level 7 and above, about 7 percent are new. Approximately 26 percent of similar level boy photographs are new (categorised as level 7 or above). In these new pictures, forty one percent of the girls and 56 percent of the boys are between the ages of 9-12, the rest being younger. The vast majority of both sexes of children depicted in the new pictures of level 7 and above are white

Caucasian, with Asiatic children more likely to appear in posed images (levels 5 and 6). There is a marked absence of black children in any of the age groups, and as yet there is little evidence as to why this should be the case. Anecdotal information from the copine interviews with offenders suggested that many show a preference for thin, fair children, where genitalia are clearly visible and where there are no secondary sexual characteristics.

Currently, photographs are appearing in the newsgroups monitored by the project at a rate of about two new children per month. This is highly variable, but there is evidence that the age of the children (particularly females) is getting younger, that there is an increase in "domestic" production (where the settings are family rooms), and that there has been a growth in the number of photographs of East European children. Over the last year, there has also been an increase in the number of pictures whose origins appear to be commercial web sites, based in South America or Eastern Europe; these pictures tend to be in levels 5 and 6. These, and the emergence of more explicit child pornography from Eastern Europe access to which involves payment, seem to represent a growth in commercial exploitation of the market for child pornography. It can be estimated that between 300-350 of the children included in the new/recent material have been subjected to serious sexual assault.

Of the 1,600-1,800 children who have been photographed while posing naked (levels 5 and 6), it is reasonable to assume that a number of these will have been sexually assaulted, either outside of being photographed or without the images being distributed. It is also reasonable to assume that the figures given here are an underestimate of the numbers of pictures in circulation as the amount of material in private circulation is currently unknown. It is important to stress that technological changes are evident in the emergence of material distributed through the Internet, but Video still seems to remain the principal primary production medium for child pornography. This is reflected in new recent Internet material in the amount of high quality video captures. The age, sex and ethnicity of the children in the copine database videos clips are very similar to the distribution found in the still pictures.

The new technologies also mean that "users" of the Internet can quickly become "producers." Such photographs do not need to be commercially processed which allows for a much greater level of security in their production. Recent cases in the United Kingdom give some indication of the extent to which this occurs. Images can also be altered by the paedophile to suit personal preferences, or can even be made up of components from separate photographs. Such images are often called "pseudo photographs."

Indeed, technology is now allowing the creation of lifelike child pornography without the use of children at all. The Internet also allows for on-line abuse of children. In 1996, a group of paedophiles that called itself the Orchid Club was arrested in the United States. Using a digital camera, one of the group members transmitted real-time images of a child being sexually assaulted and responded to requests from the club's members in directing the abuse. Members of the Orchid club lived in the United States, Europe and Australia. A major source for both text and images are the Usenet Newsgroups. There are some 30,000 such groups on the Internet covering a wide range of subjects (the vast majority of which are innocent and appropriate) but paedophiles use some of these newsgroups to communicate with each other, to ask advice about computer-related problems or the availability of new software. They also use them to request pictures from other paedophiles and to post them.

The pictures in themselves act as a form of currency, legitimizing activity and creating social cohesion. Bulletin Board Systems (bbs) are similar to Newsgroups but with more real time involvement. Web based bbss have played an increasingly important role in the on-line paedophile community in recent years. Durkin and Bryant talk of them as high tech party lines, by which users can send and receive text, engage in conversations, and both upload and download files. A more familiar means of communication is through e-mail and the mass distribution of e-mail files through List Servers (Listservs). A further important source of both information and material is Internet Relay Chat (irc). This is a vast multiuser discussion forum, which allows users to communicate through text but in real time. Paedophiles in irc can exchange files directly with one another using a Direct Client-to-Client (dcc) feature and can distribute images through Fserves. This allows the user to access a certain part of another user's hard drive to upload and download files. Paedophiles can therefore be invited to 'visit' somebody else's collection and take what material they want.

The World Wide Web (WWW) is another source of child pornography. It is now relatively easy to create Web pages and features built into Web browsers enable users to capture content created by other people with a minimum of effort. The proliferation of free web servers has meant that individuals can upload a web site containing child pornography anonymously, and with ease. It is unknown how many people look at child pornography on the Internet, nor is it always clear what motivates them to do so. Out of the many thousands of people who simply look, there are a much smaller number who are involved in the distribution or production of material, or both. This ongoing series of interviews includes downloaders (no assault); downloaders and assault (no production); downloaders and distribution (no assault), downloaders and producers (assaults); downloaders, producers and distributors (assaults); sexual assaults only.

The Copine Project used a thematic analysis was used to establish a broad framework for understanding the data, followed by a more discursive analysis to look at how individuals negotiate their accounts. Emergent themes from the interviews illustrated that people who use the Internet to download pornography move through a series of stages in their offending behaviour which is directly influenced by their level of engagement with the Internet. Setting events for downloading included histories of early sexualised behaviour, inadequate adult socialization, dissatisfaction with current persona and an acquisition of computer and Internet skills. Initial contact with the Internet was often accompanied by accessing adult pornographic sites before a search for child pornography. Accessing such material facilitates engagement with a virtual community, further normalizing the collection of material, as well as promoting further engagement with the Internet and its corresponding technology.

For all people interviewed, this was followed by a steady increase in on-line behaviour and a reduction in other outside social engagement. Increasingly large quantities of material are rapidly collected, and what emerges are different forms of collecting behaviour, with time spent sorting and cataloguing images. Such categories might be quite rudimentary, organized around age or sex of the children photographed, or more sophisticated with a focus on content of activities. For those people who download and go on to engage in social contacts on the Internet, the process of sustaining that engagement requires credibility. Such credibility is often achieved through the exchange or trade of material such as pictures, text or fantasy stories.

The process of collecting appears to be an important psychological process in itself. The rapid acquisition of images largely goes hand-in-hand with the acquisition of technical skills. Collecting also leads to an increase in fantasy and sexual activity, particularly masturbation in relation to images or through engaging in mutual fantasies with others while on-line. With increasing mastery of the Internet comes also a sense of power and control, and this is also evidenced in some of the preferred fantasy material about "teaching" children about love and sex. Where downloaders also communicate with each other, this becomes a powerful justification for their activity, and there is constant reference to the importance of on-line relationships over material. For downloaders who trade images, the notion of photographs as currency is important. They are currency in terms of trading for new images, but they are also currency in maintaining existing on-line relationships and giving credibility. Text never exclusively replaces images, but for many downloaders it seems to play an important role in the process of engagement, and may enable the formation of close relationships, some of which move from being "virtual" to "real."

The appeals of the Internet for those with a sexual interest in children are many. Social connections can vastly increase, and such virtual communities, while providing a safe haven, also allow for the control of social distance and intimacy. The Internet allows the user to achieve a sense of mastery on-line, and status and prestige are achieved by those with good computer skills. Such skills, and the ability to master the virtual environment provide a sense of power. Users gain social confidence while on-line and report that they find it easier to make friends, using the metaphor of the Internet as the Prozac of social communication. There is also the suggestion of altered states of consciousness through Internet use, facilitating levels of engagement that would otherwise be seen as aversive or inappropriate.

The appeal of the Internet is problematic in relation to sexual interest in children. Paradoxically, Internet use among offenders increases socialization by providing a potentially enormous virtual community, while at the same time reducing the number of real social contacts. This functions in a way that allows for the normalization of sexual interest in children and enables engagement through the reduction in outside social contacts that might otherwise challenge the acceptability of the interest. It also functions in a way that allows the avoidance of personal responsibility by creating anonymity, facilitating identity choices and movement through identities. With regard to sexual behaviour, the Internet lowers sexual inhibitions and the engagement in the sharing or trading of images acts as a form of social reinforcement.

The ability to manipulate the images to fit a sexual fantasy further makes an object of the child and enables control of the source of stimulation. Knowledge of the risks being taken in downloading material can also serve to heighten arousal. Like all other offenders, people who download child pornography are able to legitimize their activity, and the role of the virtual Internet community in generating such a body of legitimizing stories appears to be important. Offenders talk of a lack of any objective measure as to whether the child in the picture was actually being abused, or relate their own experience of abuse.

A frequent comment refers to the smiling faces of the children in the pictures, as proof of their enjoyment, or personal fantasies of abuse that normalize the process of collecting. Whatever the level of participation in such a "community," the process of obtaining photographs through the Internet validates and legitimizes such activity and provides a sense of support to those with a sexual interest in children. Such an engagement is flexible and dynamic and offenders can engage at multiple levels through different kinds of self-representation. While those who access child pornography through the Internet evidence many similarities with other child sex offenders, they also demonstrate varying measures of "functional addiction," such as salience, mood modification, tolerance, withdrawal symptoms and conflict and relapse. This is an important consideration in the development of both appropriate assessment and treatment programs for offenders.

There are a number of concerns that arise out of the Copine Project. Despite the temptation of putting resources into the detection of the relatively easier offences of possession and trading, the emphasis must also be on child protection and the identification of children. Training for law enforcement and other professionals needs to address the evidential issues relating to the pictures, with emphasis on tracing the chain of postings and seeing the picture content as evidential forensic material. To understand the processes involved requires knowledge of the behaviour of downloaders and the language they use. These concerns are echoed in assumptions made about current treatment for such offenders and whether they are sufficiently similar to other sex offenders to be included in the same programs.

Through net experiences people have come to reinterpret society, relationships and the self. The possibility that people are changed by and subsequently contribute to change through the Internet is highly relevant to the area of sexual offending. Through the Internet we see a potential change in the offender's beliefs, values and cognitive styles. The fact that through the Internet users can in the main go anywhere and say anything without any official governing body restricting those actions means that for some people this will be their first experience of acting outside the confines of a conventional hierarchy. The important observation that "conventional hierarchies are disrupted by a distributed, decentralised network in which power is spread among various people and groups and one voice does not dominate or pre-empt others." Such experiences may empower some people such as sex offenders who have otherwise felt marginalised in conventional society.

6

Early Childhood Education

The availability and affordability of high quality early childhood care and education (ECCE) services significantly affect school-age children's outcomes. When children receive high quality ECCE, they subsequently come to school better prepared to learn and are more likely to complete primary and secondary school.

Current Trends of ECCE

This section discusses the ways in which the availability of ECCE for children 0 to 5 may significantly affect whether other children who are 6 to 14 can attend school and study regularly. It will review the findings from a series of ongoing studies conducted as part of The Project on Global Working Families that begin to illuminate the impact on school-age children of inadequate ECCE. The project had analysed large household surveys from nations in Latin America, Africa, Asia, North America, and Europe to investigate the impact on school-age children's educational opportunities of the need to provide care for 0-5 year olds. The conducted complementary analyses of national household and local level in-depth interviews in diverse countries. Together, these studies suggest the following.

— When parents of children 6-14 years old work, their children are more likely to go to school. Increased family income from work makes it more affordable for parents to pay school fees, buy uniforms and books, and defray the extra costs that often even attending state schools incurs. Moreover, an increase in parental earnings makes it less likely that children themselves will have to work for pay so families can afford such basic necessities as food, shelter, and clothing.

— While parental work in general increases the likelihood that all children in a household will attend school, when parents of young children (0-5) have to work and have no affordable ECCE available, children 6-14 may be taken out of school to care for younger siblings, cousins, and other children in the family.

— While being pulled out of school to care for younger children affects both boys and girls, it disproportionately affects girls' enrolment.

Specifically, the analyses of data from large national surveys in Botswana, Brazil, Mexico, Russia, South Africa, and Vietnam revealed the following. In most cases, having at least one child 0-5 in a household in which all adults worked led to an increase in the probability that some children 6-14 did not attend school. The presence of 0-5 year olds in need of care decreased the probability of school attendance by 6-14 year olds in single working parent, two parent, and extended families in which all adults worked in Botswana, Mexico, and South Africa.

The presence of preschool children in need of care decreased school attendance in the majority of categories for which sufficient data were available in Brazil and Russia. One country which did not follow this pattern was Vietnam. It is noteworthy that Vietnam was the only country in which the overwhelming majority of families with school-age children surveyed (80%) lived in rural areas.

Finally, using the national data, in the four out of five countries for which sufficient data were available, it was disproportionately girls whose school attendance declined in households in which 0-5 year olds needed care. Having all adults work raised the probability of older children spending ten or more hours a week providing child care. While the findings from analysis of household survey data are suggestive, further research is needed to determine the extent to which the differences in school attendance observed in the countries other than Russia are due to caring for 0-5 year old children or to other factors.

A significant number of working parents with 0-5-year-old children rely on paid and unpaid children to provide child care. Around 43% of families with children 0-5 years old in Mexico with whom discussed child care relied on older children to care for their younger children some or all the time, as did 47% of respondents in Botswana and 36% of respondents in Vietnam. Some of this care was provided when routine care fell through-requiring older children to miss intermittent days of school, some occurred during afterschool hours-keeping older children from doing homework and leaving them to fall behind or fail in school, while in other cases older children were removed from school all-together to provide care full-time.

In every country, poor families were far more likely to have to rely on school-age children and youths to provide care for younger children than non-poor families were. In the past, policy debates have often pitted the need to invest public resources in the education of 6-14 year olds against the need to invest in ECCE for 0-5 year olds. The analysis of the best available data strongly suggests that investing in ECCE for 0-5 year olds should not be seen as competing with meeting the needs of 6-14 year olds, but rather as a complementary way to help meet the needs of older children. In short, investing in ECCE is critical to primary and secondary education for two reasons.

— ECCE directly supports the physical, social, emotional, and cognitive development of young children-thus preparing them in essential ways to succeed in primary school.

— The availability of affordable ECCE means that parents, particularly those living in poverty, do not have to take older children out of school in order to care for preschool children in the family while adults work to make ends meet.

England and Scotland and Sweden transferred national responsibility for early childhood education and care (early years services) and childcare for school-age children (school-age childcare services) from welfare to education departments. The extent of integration in each country and what it has meant for the relationship between schools and other services.

At the time of transfer early years services were poorly developed and fragmented. For example, they were divided between school-based provision (already the responsibility of the Department for Education) and 'childcare' services (the responsibility of the Department of Health). Levels of provision were low, with many types of provision and providers, mostly in the private sector. Post-1998, the close relationship between education and care has been emphasised in official documents. For example, the National Childcare Strategy says "there is no sensible distinction between good early education and care". In practice, however, further integration has been limited. Moreover in late 2002 responsibility for early education and childcare services was again divided, this time between the Department for Education and the Department for Work. Integration is most apparent in two areas.

—Government funding for early years education (for 3 and 4 year old children; compulsory schooling starts at 5 years) has been made available across all provision - schools, nurseries and family daycare - that meet certain conditions. These conditions include working with a new curriculum, the Foundation Stage, which also covers the first year of compulsory schooling and specifies 'early learning goals'.

— Regulation has been integrated and centralized: a national educational inspectorate regulates all educational and childcare services.

A recently-announced programme of 'children's centres' is intended to bring together care, education and other services—but in deprived areas only. Recently, too, legislation enables schools to adopt an extended role. For example, schools or their partner providers may establish childcare and other services. But there are no signs of an integrated 'whole day school' system developing. With the introduction of a 'childcare tax credit' and many different funding streams, public funding has increased. But the funding of services is now more complex than before. Staffing and qualifications remain fragmented.

Childcare workers are unequal in pay and training to teachers. A major theme has been inter-agency collaboration, broader than early years, school-age childcare and schools. The Government has established a Children and Young Person's Unit which is developing an "overarching strategy for all services for children and young people". A Treasury-led initiative, Sure Start, funds local programmes in disadvantaged areas, bringing together childcare, health, family support and other services for children under 4 years and their families.

Reforms in Scotland have taken place in the context of devolution and with the re-establishment of a Scottish Parliament providing more time for debate and legislation. England and Scotland still have much in common. For example, before transfer of responsibility in 1998, the structure and level of early years and school-age childcare services in Scotland were similar to England's. Both countries have increased funding for early years education, and the extent of further integration is most apparent in this area. But there are important differences of emphasis and approach. Like England, there is a curriculum spanning 3 to 6 year olds. But the Scottish 'Pre-school Curriculum' is less prescriptive than the English Foundation Stage, offering a statement of good practice with no learning goals specified. Regulation of childcare remains within welfare, although integrated inspection is being developed with education.

An important and distinctive Scottish policy is the New Community Schools Initiative. The pilot programme, launched in 1998, is now being extended to all schools. The aim is a child-centred and integrated approach to education, health and family support. Developments often involve lifelong learning, with schools linked to, or the base for, early years, school age childcare and adult learning. Another distinctive feature is that national responsibility for child welfare has been integrated within the education department, alongside schools and early years and schoolage childcare service. There is a strong emphasis on interagency collaboration.

Prior to 1996, integration was already far advanced. Most local authorities had brought together responsibility for early years services, schools and school-age childcare into one department. There was an extensive and well-funded system of early years services, already completely integrated. The integration of school-age childcare into schools, creating 'whole day schools', was already advanced, as was the transfer of 6 year olds from nurseries to school-based 'pre-school classes'. Team working in schools, involving pre-school teachers, school teachers and free-time pedagogues, was widespread. Clusters of services—early years, school-age childcare and schools— were increasingly managed by a rektor, who could come from any of the above professions.

Since the national transfer of responsibility from welfare to education departments in 1996, educational principles have been extended to early years and school-age childcare services. There is a universal entitlement to these services for children aged 1 to 12 years. All services now have curricula: one for early years services, another covering schools and school-age childcare. A period of free attendance for 4 and 5 year olds has been introduced. Most radical of all, training for staff in early years services, schools and school-age childcare services has been unified.

The integration process has differed considerably in the three countries, reflecting different histories, contexts and policy agendas. Sweden already had a coherent, developed system of universal services, in both welfare and education. 'Childcare for working parents' had been achieved and levels of child poverty were low. Neither was a major policy issue. In these conditions, Swedish reforms have been educationally focused, aiming for a common approach across services, with shared understandings of learning, care and childhood. Integration is underpinned by a strong holistic pedagogical tradition, summed up in Sweden's pre-school curriculum: "the pre-school should provide children with good pedagogical activities, where care, nurturing and learning together form a coherent whole". By contrast, the integration process in England and Scotland has taken place in the context of a strong welfare policy agenda focused on reducing high levels of poverty and increasing employment. Priority has been given to increasing 'childcare for working parents'.

Traditions and policy principles that might support the integration of care and education are lacking. For example, there is no concept like 'pedagogy'; while policy is based on limited, targeted public intervention for childcare and universal publicly-funded provision for education. A plethora of services and providers and a market-approach in care and education are further obstacles to developing integrated services. The situation in Scotland is far closer to England than Sweden, with a strong welfare focus. However, there is a greater emphasis on social inclusion, as opposed to reducing exclusion. Programmes such as New Community Schools offer a more universalist vision.

In all three countries, integration has focused attention on compulsory schooling, and its relationship with other services. Is it possible to create a 'strong and equal relationship' In England and Scotland an 'equal relationship' has been made more difficult by a 'mixed economy' of public, private and nonprofit services and some tension between the promotion of schools as community resources and market-oriented policies that emphasise parents' right to choose schools.

The experience of these three countries raises several other issues. Wide-ranging integration requires re-thinking as well as re-structuring. An inherently integrative concept like pedagogy supports rethinking and provides a strong foundation. Lastly, integration is made harder if the services involved have strongly differing values, principles and purposes.

Impacts on HIV/AIDS Control

The HIV epidemic has transformed the childhood, youth and adulthood of millions globally. Over three million children and 38 million adults are infected with HIV worldwide. The epidemic affects early childhood both through the illness and death of children themselves and through the illness and death of parents, teachers, and other caretakers. While the footprint of the HIV pandemic is felt globally, the impact is currently greatest in the southern cone of Africa.

In the last year alone, there were 3.5 million new HIV infections among adults and children in sub-Saharan Africa. Yet countries well beyond Africa are affected. Recently, attention has been focused on the rapid rise of infection rates in Asia and in Central and Eastern Europe. In Eastern Europe and Central Asia, 1.2 million adults and children are living with HIV. India has 4 million infected adults and children, a total second only to South Africa. By 2010, if current trends continue, 10 million Chinese could be infected with HIV. While new programs to increase the availability of treatment in resource-poor countries bring new hopes for longer survival for those who are HIV-infected, the availability of medications is only one essential part of what is needed.

One of the most important challenges for those nations that already have high infection rates is how to raise healthy children while at the same time addressing the needs of those adults and children who are already infected. For a number of countries, this challenge is particularly urgent. In South Africa, an estimated 20% of reproductive age adults are infected, in Zimbabwe 34%, in Botswana 39%, in Swaziland 33%, in Lesotho 31%, in Namibia 23%, in Zambia 22%, and in Malawi 15%.

Parents who are HIV caregivers compared to non HIV care givers, are significantly more likely to report that they are worried about the quality of child care their children receive (53% versus 34%). Their worries stem from concern about their children receiving adequate care when the children are sick. 75% of parents who are HIV caregivers worried that their children would not receive adequate care when their children were sick.

In the absence of adequate child care for HIV-infected children when they become sick, parents often are the ones who must provide this care. As a result, they frequently leave work to attend to sick children. Among parents who are HIV caregivers, 29 per cent leave work at least once per month to attend to sick children compared to only 19% of parents who were not HIV caregivers. The need to be absent from work to provide care for sick children frequently led to loss of income and at times led to job loss. Both could result in serious implications for families' ability to care adequately for their young children as the loss of income led them deeper into poverty.

Young children who are not HIV-infected themselves are often still deeply affected by the epidemic-both when their parents become sick and when their parents have to care for others who are sick. HIV care giving affects the ability of parents to provide routine care for children who are not infected. Parents who are HIV caregivers spent an average of 74 hours per month providing care to their children, 22 hours less than non-caregivers. The amount of time they needed to be working as HIV caregivers substantially reduced their availability to their own children. 48% of HIV caregivers spent two or less hours per day with their own children.

Several important policy considerations arise out of what are beginning to learn about the impact of HIV on families with young children. In particular, there are implications for the quantity and nature of early childhood care and education services needed and the supports necessary to enable parents and extended family members to care for children who are HIV-infected and affected.

First, we need to markedly increase the supply of

early childhood care and education in the countries with the highest rates of HIV. Many parents who previously cared for young children at home are no longer able to because of illness or death. At the same time, the necessity of the surviving parents to work, or in the case where both parents have died, the need of extended family members to work, is increasing the demand for early childhood care and education. Moreover, the amount of time healthy parents have available to be the primary or sole caregiver of young children is declining because of the amount of time they have to spend as HIV caregivers.

Second, HIV is changing the nature of early childhood care demanded. Children who are HIV-infected and affected face both increased health and developmental challenges. To address these substantial challenges, we will need to increase the ability of early childhood care providers to care for children when they have illnesses and developmental problems and to increase the ability of parents and other guardians to get paid leave from work so that they can provide care for children when early childhood care providers cannot. Both of these measures are feasible.

Both through the use of on-site health care professionals and social workers and by bringing children to nearby public services, residential care programs in southern Africa already help care for the physical and mental health of children who have been orphaned or whose parents are too ill to provide care themselves. It will be less expensive for day care programs than residential ones to provide this same critical support to HIV-infected and affected children living in the community. Increasing the availability of paid leave, an ingredient key to parents' and guardians' roles, is also feasible.

Twenty African countries, like many other countries throughout the world, already provide in their labor codes or public policies for employees to receive paid leave for their own health. These policies need to be adjusted so that paid sick leave can be taken for family illnesses as well as the employee's. South Africa already has a policy of providing employees with paid leave for child sickness or family death. While African nations currently face the highest HIV prevalence rates, these policy changes are equally needed in all regions of the world. They would provide a critical step forward for those working globally in the formal sector. Parallel initiatives to make leave affordable for those working in the informal sector need to be developed.

Caring for the health and development of young HIV-infected and affected children will increasingly be shared by early childhood care providers and the children's families. It is only through their combined efforts that children will be able to receive adequate care and parents and other guardians will be able to work and earn the income needed to survive. It is clear that the overall need for quality early childhood care services is increasing as a result of HIV. Not only is there a need for greater supply, but it is also necessary for these services to adapt to meet the new demands of HIV-infected and affected children.

Early childhood care services can play an essential role in helping families and societies survive the HIV pandemic. At the same time, parents and other caregivers of HIV-infected and affected children need the working conditions and workplace supports that make it possible for them to truly partner in this crucial task.

The field of Early Childhood goes by various names, in different countries as well as within individual countries, where different stakeholders may use different references. Nor do international agencies have a commonly agreed-upon term, sparking debate when an inter-agency document is drafted over which name to use. Researchers have tried to unify the field with a single label, but without success. Primary education also has different names, but unlike with Early Childhood, there is a relatively common understanding of what it refers to and the way in which it is delivered.

The terms attached to Early Childhood go beyond mere labels: they imply different purposes, pedagogical practices and forms of delivery, not to mention the varying social and economic status of the personnel involved. The variety of terms is so broad that the very identity of Early Childhood as a distinctive discipline is often questioned. One commonly used name, Early Childhood Education (ECE), is favoured by education authorities or others who are inclined to see early childhood from an educational point of view. Learning is central to this tradition. Early Childhood Care and Education (ECCE) is an expansion of ECE, with the care component added. Or the order can be changed to Early Childhood Education and Care (ECEC) to keep the emphasis on education. Then there is Early Childhood Care (ECC) without the education component. In the developing world, ECC tends to be associated with attention to the child's health, nutrition and hygiene, while in the developed world, it is often understood as a social service for working mothers with young children.

Historically, ECC has also been associated with institutionalised social services for disadvantaged children, whereas ECE has been considered a service devoted to the child's early learning process. In an effort to assert the inseparability of ECC and ECE, researchers have coined the word Educare. But this term has remained mainly within the academic community and has not entered the policy discourse of governments. Early Childhood Development (ECD) is another term whose popularity is increasing. It emphasises a holistic approach attending to the child's physical, emotional, social as well as cognitive development. Though elusive, by being comprehensive, and focusing on the child, not on the social agent or on the process of care or education, ECD is gaining ground as one of the most generic terms for the field. A common variant of this term is Early Childhood Care and Development (ECCD), which again tries to span the divide between care and development/ education. Yet another variant is Early Childhood Care for Development which places the emphasis on the care which affects development and learning.

Several other terms are in use, but they are either variations or different combinations of the three key concepts—early childhood care, development and education—or specific programmes that are arranged for them (e.g., pre-school education for ECE). From the child development perspective, these three concepts cannot be treated independently of one another. Early child development encompasses a series of learning processes during which the child learns about the environment and himself/herself. That the child's survival and growth has to be assured by appropriate provision of health and nutritional care goes without saying. But the young child's physical growth should also be accompanied by an appropriate learning process. Learning and growth cannot occur in sequence. They are integral parts of the process of nurturing a child's holistic development. In reality, ECC, ECD, and ECE are not invariably institutionalised or practised separately. For instance, one can easily find a Department of Early Childhood Education responsible for the entire gamut of early childhood programmes including day care centres for children under three and kindergarten education for older children. In most of the developed countries, kindergarten education is child-centred, stressing the child's holistic development. In such cases, the need for a distinction between ECE and ECD would not arise.

In some countries in transition, pre-school education is a generic term for early childhood programmes including those for children under three, which would be categorised as ECC in other countries. Different labels become an issue in institutional politics. For agencies, the preference for one term over another is closely linked to the institutional mandate they are expected to fulfil. Such discrepancies that exist among agencies—not their understanding of child psychology or development—are often difficult to reconcile. At the country level, the education ministry may prefer ECE because it is easier to justify involvement and investment in education rather than in the care of small children. If the ministry makes a distinction between ECE and ECC or ECD, it may be because it intends to assign different responsibilities to the different areas. In this regard, it is no mere coincidence that in some developing countries ECD is often accompanied by community mobilisation strategies soliciting contributions from the community, while ECE gets priority in government funding. Educators working outside the field of ECE are less likely to be called teachers, since such a label would imply a certain level of remuneration by the government, which is unavailable, in most developing countries. Given the multifaceted nature of early childhood, the existence of several labels may be inevitable.

The range of the institutional interests is such that it may, in fact, be a futile attempt to seek a unifying label. Meanwhile, the same term or name can be interpreted differently in different social, cultural and linguistic contexts. And depending on school starting age, the concept of early childhood, or 'early childhood' as a policy construct varies. Thus comparing, let alone unifying, different names may be an elusive effort. In this regard, insistence on a common name may not be a constructive effort and what is needed would be an understanding of the common scope of Early Childhood. In making international comparisons, what is crucial would be an operational definition that can characterise countries' policies regardless of the terms being used.

More importantly, the focus on names for Early Childhood may divert attention from other equally important issues, such as how early childhood services, however they may be called, are related to other educational and social services for school age children. But labelling aside, certain fundamentals stand out.

— The ultimate concern of any early childhood programme should be the wellbeing and holistic development of the child, and regardless of the institutional setting, the programme should embody a developmentally appropriate practice, which attends to health, nutrition, security and learning. In fact, as long as such a holistic approach is practised, the physical or institutional setting of a programme is of little importance.

— As children grow, they can move from one programme to another that may be named differently or located in different ministries. But the programmes must maintain between them a pedagogical, if not necessarily an institutional, continuity and integrity.

- Overlap between differently named programmes for the same age group must be co-ordinated as much as possible. Such overlap can cause administrative inefficiency and be wasteful of resources.
- But not least, regardless of what label is accorded, the programme preceding a child's primary education should be designed to facilitate the child's preparation for and transition to formal schooling.

Pedagogical continuity between the last year of an early childhood programme and the first year of formal schooling is of great importance. The issue of labelling is not purely conceptual to be discussed from the point of view of child development theories. Rather, it is inextricably related, among others, to institutional responsibilities and the mandates of the stakeholders involved, which cannot be handled effectively without a clear policy stance on Early Childhood. Preparing a government-wide position or a position that can be subscribed to by all stakeholders vis-à-vis the labels to be used may be a good starting point for policy development for Early Childhood.

Status of Working Women's Children

Most female workers in developing countries, particularly in Asia-Pacific and Africa, do not have wage jobs. Female workers in these regions work mostly in agriculture, with a status of unpaid family worker. In Sub-Saharan Africa, the majority of the economically active female population is in agriculture (68%). In Asia and the Pacific, this trend is more pronounced the lower the income level of the country, with about 78% of female workers in least developed countries in the region employed in agriculture. According to available data on employment status in some developing countries, female workers engaged in wage jobs make up less than 10%. The preponderance of female workers in non-wage jobs, however, is not consistent across all developing countries.

In Latin America and the Caribbean, the proportion of women who are unpaid family workers has dropped considerably, with most female workers now either wage earners or selfemployed. But a burgeoning informal sector for female workers in this region suggests that female workers counted as having wage status may in fact not be in regular employee situations, but in non-core situations, such as those working from home or domestic and casual workers. The proportion of non-wage female workers in developing countries is assumed to be greater than suggested by available data. In most countries, statistics on the informal sector come solely from urban areas, and many rural women working informally are not counted. Furthermore, most women in developing countries are engaged in economic activities that do not normally figure in labour statistics or are not recognised as work at all, such as subsistence agriculture and housework. Although these activities are vital to society and to household economy, they have no recognised market value.

The main conclusions from these observations are, first, that mothers in the developing world cannot be assumed to be freely available to serve as full-time child caretakers and, second, that the demand for ECCE-FBS is huge among working mothers in developing countries.

This demand, however, is hidden. In order to motivate governments to increase their involvement and investment in ECCE-FBS, this hidden demand must be exposed. To this end, labour force statistics should be made more gender-sensitive; specifically, by assigning market values to non-wage jobs and unpaid family work-to the goods and services women produce at home. Data should also be available to show that mothers performing non-wage work are not fully available for childcare functions. The irony is that despite their difficulties, mothers in non-wage jobs, especially little educated rural mothers engaged in agricultural work, tend to combine work and family responsibilities more often than those in wage jobs.

Many of these women simply have no other choice, but their carrying of the double burden perpetuates the myth that "stay-at-home" mothers are available to take care of children and have no particular need for ECCE-FBS. These observations have a few implications for ECCEFBS policy in developing countries.

— Family support measures such as parental leave, granted in developed countries to parents of young children under age two, are unlikely to be available in developing countries, at least in the near future. The reason is that apart from obvious obstacles such as resource constraints, governments in developing countries have difficulty delivering such family support to the target population because of the technical problem of mapping the presence of mothers and fathers working in the informal sector in the absence of contractual arrangements. Parental leave systems require a sophisticated administration system tracking the parents' employment conditions and status.

— Given a relatively high per-child cost, institutional services for children under three are also out of reach in most developing countries. As far as the care and education of young children in their first years is concerned, one feasible option is to educate parents in the basics of cleaning, feeding and interacting with children. Parent education, which does not require a sophisticated administration system, as it can be delivered non-formally, can have a substantial positive impact on early childhood development by making parents more effective early childhood educators. Parent education does not help solve the problem of the parents' non-availability but it makes them become more effective early childhood educators when available.

Mothers in disadvantaged situations, the main target population of parent education programmes, are not easily available to attend classes. For this reason, home-based programmes have been devised to mobilise mothers to serve as collective early childhood educators for groups of children in neighbourhood communities. Such an approach allows mothers to work while their children are under the care of someone with at least a minimum of training. However, home-based and parent education programmes should not be considered permanent alternatives to government spending on professional care and education for disadvantaged children. In addition, in order to ensure quality, these programmes, too, require government support and involvement to build the necessary administrative infrastructure.

Finally, in the long term, investment in the education of girls and women will have a synergistic effect on the development of ECCE-FBS. Mothers' education levels have been shown to have a negative correlation with their fertility rates: educated mothers produce fewer children. Smaller families in turn allow the government to increase per-child expenditures for early childhood services, thereby improving access and quality. Educated mothers do not require extensive parent education, nor do they need to be convinced of its importance as much as uneducated mothers do. Furthermore, educated mothers are far more likely to be employed in the formal sector, and their presence as visible contributors to the economy increases the perceived demand for ECCE-FBS and prompts the government to deliver FBS services.

Government investment is a political decision arising from the determination of priorities. To trigger it, demand must be clearly communicated. Dire statistics on child development (e.g., infant mortality) may reveal the need for ECCE-FBS, but need alone, unfortunately, is not enough to win government investment. While mothers are not the sole beneficiaries of ECCE-FBS, they are the strategic beneficiaries in the sense that their voice can communicate the demand. In this regard, encouraging women, through good education, to participate more actively in the formal labour market is not only a sound economic strategy, but also a good strategy for ECCEFBS. Likewise, investment in ECCE-FBS to reinforce positive child development is a sound economic strategy, given that it will translate into long-term savings on remedial social and educational programmes.

Impacts of Cross-sectoral Co-ordination

Early childhood care and education is the concern of many government sectors, notably the education, social affairs and health sectors. Co-ordination among these sectors in policy development and implementation is essential for ensuring the child's holistic development and the efficient use of government resources. Coherent regulation, funding and staffing schemes as well as a common vision of care and education among the concerned sectors are key factors that determine the quality of early childhood programmes.

Cross-sectoral co-ordination is difficult, however, especially at the national level. It is one of the main challenges facing many governments of both developed and developing countries wishing to promote a holistic approach to early childhood. Responses to the challenge have varied from one country to another. Some have sought to remove the problem at the structural level by integrating the area into a single ministry. This is a trend in some developed countries. Others have tried to divide sectoral responsibilities according to age range. But most have opted for the less dramatic approach of seeking coherence in policy and administration through co-ordination mechanisms (COMs).

In general, COMs are effective when their function is to co-ordinate a particular early childhood programme. For instance, in 2000 the Government of Singapore, seeking to co-ordinate pre-school education programmes provided by both the Ministry of Education and the Ministry of Community Development and Sports, set up a Pre-school Education Steering Committee, with the MOE designated as the lead ministry. With input from the Committee, to date a common kindergarten curriculum framework has been launched to be used by both services and a Kindergarten Bill is being prepared. Through another joint committee, the two ministries have also successfully developed a joint training framework for pre-school teachers and accredited training courses and trainers for the required preschool training courses, important steps towards the country's development of a common system of pre-school teacher training to improve the quality of teachers. A COM that focuses on the same target population also seems to encourage convergence and co-operation between different sectors.

A case in point is the National Coordination and Technical Committee of the Programme Opportunities in Mexico. The mechanism was instrumental in delivering to extremely poor families an integrated social assistance programme incorporating education, health and nutrition components. "The delivery of particular services continues to be the responsibility of each sector, but a concerted effort is made to see that these services get to the same population, thereby trying to take advantage of the synergistic effects such as concentration or convergence." The Committee's success has also been attributed to the fact that its members, coming from all the relevant sectors, jointly set the rules of operation and approve new initiatives. A COM also seems to be effective in carrying out a specific task for a certain period of time.

While COMs have been effective in co-ordinating sectors to handle specific programmes and tasks, they have not been very successful in promoting a coherent overall policy and administrative framework across sectors. This in part has to do with their ad hoc status. In an effort to maintain sectoral neutrality, the COM is often set up as an ad hoc body outside of a line ministry, with no decisionmaking authority. Such COMs can, at best, make recommendations to ministries, but most have proven to have little influence with ministries, especially regarding decisions related to policy changes and funding, unless as in the U.K. example the mechanism made recommendations that were solicited at the lead sector's initiative. To counteract the lack of authority, COMs are often affiliated with a high political office (e.g., president, prime minister, first lady). Such political affiliation certainly helps increase visibility and ability to command cooperation. But political patronage can have a price: when the government changes, the COM also undergoes a "transformation". In most cases, it is dismantled; if it stays in place, its functions and mandate are altered or diminished, disrupting continuity.

Similarly, high-level membership is often suggested to reinforce the authority of COMs. The involvement of authorities with the necessary decision-making power and commitment is, of course, crucial. But when high-level authorities are asked to take part in a mechanism that does not handle issues or decisions requiring their level of authority, they tend to delegate the responsibility to junior staff. This delegation process has been found to be time consuming, and the selected staff members are often less committed and less likely to attend meetings than members of a mechanism set up as a technical body appropriate to their level of functioning. The delegation process can even cause the mechanism to fail, simply through the difficulty of convening meetings among members. One structural way to ensure the COM's decision-making power is to place it under a line ministry. This strategy requires the designation of a lead sector—a challenging prospect for early childhood services.

— Singling out a sector can be risky, no matter how necessary, if the government has not already clearly associated early childhood with that particular sector, as the decision can inadvertently diminish the roles of the other sectors.

— The choice of a lead sector is a decision that hinges on many factors. It varies, understandably, with the ideological context as well as the particular early childhood priorities of the country. There is no one-size fits-all approach; each country must go through its own consultative, reflective and learning processes.

— Once a sector is designated, it must be open to a comprehensive approach, embracing the concerns of all the sectors involved and mobilising their respective strengths and competences.

But balancing leadership and partnership is not facile and not many countries, especially those in the developing region where early childhood has not been part of the government's public policy, have mastered the art. Despite these challenges, making one sector responsible for co-ordination is necessary if a COM is to be functional, especially if the mechanism aims to bring about changes at the policy and administrative levels. Unlike other functions expected of a COM, to develop and implement a coherent early childhood policy and administration system requires more than merely bringing different sectors together. There must be a clear understanding of where the coordination is to be centred, and more importantly the identified leader should be able to exercise the necessary authority, while mustering a partnership with all the sectors involved. This eventually amounts to the importance of a national decision on the lead sector for early childhood, without which even a compromise, moderate measure such as setting up a COM will not generally be very effective.

Early Learning Practises: The US Experience

In USA, early education and out-of-school time have increasingly been promoted as the best investment to ensure that all children succeed in K-12 school. Currently, parents bear sole responsibility for creating the link between early learning and out-of-school programs and K-12 schools. Yet they often lack adequate information about typical child development and guidelines for K-12 education. While States, through their local school districts, are held directly responsible for children's learning, they are not maximizing significant potential gains from improving the quality of a child's education prior to Kindergarten and during the student's time out-of-school. In achieving the goals of the state's Basic Education Act which include knowledge, problem-solving skills, and work preparedness, the Child Care Coordinating Committee (CCCC) can be an active partner to the Administration, the Legislature, and the Office of the Superintendent of Public Instruction to articulate the need for and benefits of strong linkages among early educators, out-of-school time programs, and K-12 schools in order to align early education and out-of-school time with K-12 learning. The CCCC examines the issue of School Readiness and School Success with the goal of building a bridge of educational opportunities from birth to adulthood.

Increasingly, educators and policy makers at the national, state, and local levels agree that a child's readiness for school depends upon his/her experiences outside of the K-12 school day. These experiences include the learning that takes place in the child's family, early care and education, and the youth's time out-of-school.

Eight educational goals, including the goal that all children begin school "ready to learn" by the Year 2000, have been established at the national level by National Education Goals Panel. The panel outlined three components of school readiness:

— His/her physical health and small/large motor development

— Social and emotional development

— Approaches to learning

— Language development

— Cognitive skills and learning

— School's readiness for children

— Smooth transition between home and school

— Continuity between early childhood education programs and elementary schools

— Helping children understand a complex world

— Commitment to the success of every child

— Commitment to the success of every teacher and adult who works with the child during the day

— Approaches that enhance a child's achievement

— Learning from and improving upon school performance

— Serving children in the community

— Responsibility for results

— Strong leadership

Support in family and community that contributes to the child's readiness

— Universal access to high-quality, developmentally appropriate early care and education

— Supporting parents as a child's first teacher

— Nutrition and physical care for all children

Similar concepts and elements are used within the Washington State. The Office of the Superintendent of Public Instruction (OSPI) promotes the dual mission of Ready Schools and Ready Children. The OSPI outlines the specifics elements that contribute to school success, which are parallel to those identified by the National Goals Panel. The Early Childhood Education and Assistance Program, a State programme created to improve school readiness among low-income preschool children, promotes the same definition as the National Goal Panel with comprehensive services and performance standards across seven competency areas.

However, national research on Kindergarten transitions indicates that almost half of entering Kindergarten students have moderate to serious problems in their transition, which is consistent with estimates from school districts in Washington State. "Kindergarten teachers have reported that the single greatest challenge they face is that a majority of the children lack some or all of the needed social and emotional competencies needed to learn". Young children who do not have the opportunities to engage in stimulating cognitive activities and nurturing social-emotional relationships are already behind their peers when they enter Kindergarten." States report that between 20 and 49 percent of all Kindergarteners begin school with delayed socialemotional development. Ensuring children's success depends upon high quality early learning, health and mental health services, and early intervention. Bipartisan consensus has emerged at the national level on the definition of a child's readiness, a school's readiness, and the community support needed for school success.

Bridge-Building Strategies

Like the blocks of concrete used to support the spans of a bridge, the support system for all educational programs is an interrelated structure. This infrastructure includes research on best practice with technical assistance, teacher training and education, high quality educational settings, and professional referrals. In the perfect world, the infrastructure would carry each child from one supportive educational environment to the next with the social, emotional, physical, and cognitive skills needed for the next level. In addition, the infrastr ucture would ensure that each educational setting would be buoyed up by resources from governmental and community-based agencies adequate to provide highquality educational experiences to each child from birth to adulthood.

Expanding upon themes from national and state initiatives, the Child Care Coordinating Committee recommends three avenues of action:

— Bolster support to parents and other early educators;

— Build partnerships among parents, early care and education, K-12 schools, and out-of-school time programs to effectively reinforce developmentally appropriate learning at all stages; and

— Align activities and outcomes in early education, K-12 schools, and programs during out-of-school time to support the full range of a child's development and achieve state learning goals.

Bolster support to parents and other early educators: Current structure of early education has been described as a "nonsystem" that lacks an overarching plan or blueprint for improvement. Incrementally, small pieces to the system have been added as pilot programs with short-term funding that generally reaches only a few parents, teachers, and other caregivers like grandparents, friends, and neighbors. As a result, the "system" addresses many elements to improve the quality of care, but only in small pieces. Without a blueprint with the end goal of universal access to high quality care, the system will continue to be fragmented. The State of Washington needs greater assurances of the universal quality of early education and out-of-school time to maximize student's success in K-12 education. Instead, efforts to build universal quality took a step backwards when Washington State child care programs and services received budget cuts of $22.3 million in State Fiscal Year 2002. These cuts represented 41 percent of the total budget reduction to the Work First program. These budget reductions impair lowincome parents' ability to retain their jobs, reduce learning opportunities for lowincome children, and increase the number of children who enter school at a disadvantage.

To prepare children for school and schools for children, the infrastructure for early learning and out-of-school care needs to be restored and enhanced.

Restore and enhance (1) continuing education and training programs for teachers and providers, (2) teacher career track and compensation programs, and (3) innovative financing initiatives, among other existing elements of the infrastructure.

Build partnerships among parents, learning settings outside school, and K-12 schools: In addition to bolstering support to parents, Washington State needs to build upon local initiatives that solidify connections among early educators, out-of-school time programs, and K-12 schools. To make progress in students' skill levels, K-12 learning urgently needs formal ties to early education and out-ofschool time programs. Parents and educators need to develop a common understanding of developmentally appropriate outcomes at each stage. Currently, a few efforts exist, primarily supported with federal funds or private grants. However, no long-term support exists to establish and institutionalize these relationships and provide parents with support in helping their children navigate the transition to Kindergarten. With each year of unsuccessful transitions, elementar y school students fall further behind.

Several promising initiatives in Washington State could be built into broader approaches. Grouped into partnerships between early learning and K-12 and partnerships between K-12 and out-of-school time programs.

The OSPI Early Learning Task Force aims to: 1) increase public awareness of the importance of early learning, 2) disseminate research on elements of quality early education, 3) coordinate policies, procedures, and outcomes among early learning programs, and 4) support funding partnerships. To accomplish this mission, the Early Learning Task Force is developing a 5-year strategic plan to support districts as they partner with early learning programs to meet state learning goals. Initiative-728, passed by the voters with a 72 percent approval rate in 2000, allows school districts to allocate funds to improve the quality of public education and create higher standards through reduced class size and other methods, including\ early assistance to students who need support prior to kindergarten and extended learning opportunities.

Based on preliminary survey data, about 16 percent of the funds have been expended on extended learning opportunities and 4 percent on expanded early learning for students at risk. School districts could use an additional portion of I-728 funds to:

a) institutionalize effective transitions from early care settings to Kindergarten and

b) support K-12 students' academic and social skills through high quality out-of-school time programs.

Washington State Project STEPS is part of a national initiative to develop collaborative statewide policies and train community teams of school districts, special education programs, child care providers, Head Start programmes, Early Childhood Education and Assistance Program, Bilingual/ Migrant programs, and families. The training, which is based on the national model developed by the University of Kentucky, builds team skills. In addition, the program develops a common language about the skills children develop in Pre-K settings and the skills that schools expect the children to have in Kindergarten.

The BOOST (Better Outcomes for Out-of-school Time) Learning Initiative is a three-year initiative funded by the Stuart Foundation under the leadership of School's Out Washington in collaboration with the Seattle Public Schools. The BOOST Learning Initiative identifies the ways that out-of-school time programs support a student's success in the classroom. In addition, School's Out Washington will aid providers to enhance their services and connect to the learning goals in the classroom. The Seattle MOST (Making the Most of Out-of-school Time) has completed the School Linkages Project, which was funded by the Wallace Reader's Digest Fund. The School Linkages Project selected six teams comprised of school representatives and out-of-school time providers to assess the needs of their community and to develop a plan of cooperative services to address those needs. The emerging partnerships were then able to launch into the Alignment Initiative, a new initiative introduced by the Seattle Public Schools that offers inkind contributions to out-of-school time programs in exchange for supporting of student's learning outcomes.

Align Learning Outcomes

From birth, children learn from adults and their environment. Although the social, emotional, and cognitive skills they develop in early education settings are critical to their future educational success, early educators and elementar y teachers do not commonly know what learning takes place in each setting. The learning outcomes from early education, K-12 schools, and out-of-school-time programs need to build upon and align with each other for students to experience smooth transitions among schools and continued educational success. In Washington and around the country, models for aligning learning outcomes are underway. Several examples are highlighted below. The strategies focus either on linking early education to K-12 schools or on creating complementary outcomes between K-12 classrooms and out-of-school-time programs. In linking early education with K-12, several states have introduced universal Pre-Kindergarten programs to ensure that children have opportunities for early education and to provide stronger linkages to school academic learning requirements.

The Washington State Board of Education established a Pre-K to 3rd Grade teacher endorsement for teacher certification in 1999. The required teacher competencies are in alignment with current research regarding learning and teaching practices for young children birth to eight years. The Office of the Superintendent of Public Instruction (OSPI) convened an Early Literacy Task Force to develop Birth to Five Frameworks for Reading, Writing, and Communication that are in alignment with the K-12 Essential Academic Learning Requirements and the grade level frameworks. The Early Literacy Task Force was comprised of a broad base of early learning stakeholders, consultants from early care and education, and K-12. This product was published in June 2000 and is currently disseminated across the state upon request through the OSPI publications department. The Birth to Five Frameworks for math has been initiated.

With a grant from the Washington State Early Childhood Education and Assistance Program (ECEAP), the Puget Sound Educational Service District created an outline that demonstrates the continuity between the developmental goals and strategies that most children develop in ECEAP/ Head Start and the State determined Essential Academic Learning Requirements for K-12. With this instrument, Head Start and ECEAP teachers and parents can understand how their children have been prepared for school, and Kindergarten teachers can be prepared for the students entering their classes.

The Maryland Model for School Readiness (MMSR)

links early education programs and local school systems to help parents, teachers, and providers support children's learning from preschool through elementary school. Teachers assess children's learning by collecting systematic portfolios of their work, communicating children's learning to parents and Kindergarten teachers, and using the assessments to modify classroom curriculum to be developmentally appropriate. In Washington D.C., all-day PreKindergarten classes are offered in every elementary school. New York State Universal PreKindergarten Program plans to offer PreKindergarten to all 4-year-olds.

Financial Gaps

In thinking about the programs that serve children and adolescents, visual images of concentric circles explain the interconnection among children, their families, the early care and out-of-school-time programs, and the community. The children and youth served by the programs in early learning and out-of-school-time range from infancy through middle school, and they spend a range of hours and varying number of days per week in the care of someone other than their parents.

The consumer families range from low to high income, with state subsidies available to very low-income families. In the next concentric circle lie the supports for the caregiver who is the teacher for that child or adolescent during child care or out-of school-time activities. There are several elements needed for an early care or out-of-school time program to meet the high quality developmental needs of the children.

Program staff: To respond to children's needs appropriately, caregivers need an educational background in typical and atypical human development, and staff with a Bachelor's degree or higher respond more appropriately to children. However, low wages for child care teachers impede a program's ability to attract and retain qualified staff. Experience combined with a solid educational background is the foundation for quality care. In the ideal system as envisioned by the Child care Coordinating Committee (CCCC), care givers complete degrees in human development or similar fields and earn salaries commensurate with equally educated human services employees.

Best practice: Currently, professional organizations and universities research and disseminate information on "best practice"—communication skills, cultural relevancy, creative environments, active curriculum, among other elements. In an ideal system, child care teachers demonstrate skills based on this research to meet the range of developmental needs of children and youth.

Referrals: Parents receive referrals to early care and out-of-school-time programs from a variety of personal and professional sources, including community-based.

Child care resource and referral programs: In an ideal system, parents simultaneously receive referrals and information about financial aid to pay for care.

Community resources: In turn, care givers and programs link families to community-based resources including health care professionals, social services, enrichment activities, and schools, all of which support healthy growth for the whole family. In an ideal system, all child care teachers access these services regularly.

Partnerships: Currently, child care programs receive in-kind support, short term grants, parent fees and donations for facilities, supplies, and staff salaries. In the ideal system, child care teachers have additional financial partners—such as parents' employers, corporations, private foundations, and government.

Transportation: Currently, very few child care programs and only some out of-school-time programs offer transportation to and from school, home, and other professional services. In an ideal system, school districts, public transportation, and early care and out-of-school-time programs would work as partners to transport children before and after school.

Funding: For funding, programmes currently rely predominantly on parent fees and government subsidies for low-income families. Ideally, public/private scholarships, endowments, and employer programmes would provide direct financial support to early care and out of school programmes and create a uniform financial aid for low and middle income families.

Facilities: Currently, child care programmes rely upon parents and in-kind donations to bring facilities up to licensing standards. Ideally, additional financial resources would be more available—for example, grants, loans, and community endowments.

The third circle represents the infrastructure, which supports individual child care, early learning, and out-of-school-time programs and refers to many the elements described above.

Knowledge base/ research: Universities and national researchers provide the theoretical base to describe best practice in caring for each child in each developmental stage.

Workforce development: Child care teachers and counselors can attend courses at colleges and through community based training organizations. Washington Stars requires minimum and annual education of lead staff, and two statewide programs and the Career and Wage Ladder Pilot Project—offer wage enhancements or bonuses to child care teachers that pursue higher education. Ideally, these programs would be available to all interested child care teachers.

Technical assistance: Technical assistance is available from local governments, community-based Child Care Resource and Referral programs, WRAP (Washington Regional Action Project) Specialists (for out-of-school-time programs), DSHS/DCCEL licensors, and peer review teams for professional accreditation.

Quality assurance: State licensors of programmes for children from infancy to 12 years of age ensure that programs operate at the minimum licensing requirements. A small, but growing percentage of child care, early learning, and out-of-school-time programs have received accreditation from national professional organizations as indicators of their quality of care.

Program information and referral services: Information and referrals come from community-based Child Care Resource and Referral programs, WRAP, and public health nurses. In an ideal system, information on financial aid would be widely available as parents seek child care and other professional support for their children.

Community linkages: Currently, early care and out-of-school-programs access various community resources, although the demand for support exceeds the available supply due to financial constraints.

Public will: Currently, parents of young children understand the importance of early care and out-of-school-time programs to building their children's self-esteem, literacy and math skills, and social skills-all of which are essential to success in early, middle, and higher education. Ideally, the concept of early education and out-of-school-time will be widely understood as a merit good one that benefits all of society by preventing school failure and crime and is supported by the tax base.

Advocacy: Advocacy organizations like Child Care Works for Washington help to educate parents as wise consumers, and to increase the public will to support healthy development among all children.

Funding strategies: Funding strategies weave themselves throughout all the above elements. Ideally, the ten-year plan will provide financial support for all these elements.

All the elements of the infrastructure must work together to support individual child care and out-of-school-time child care teachers and programs to meet the needs of the children and youth in their care.

At every tier of the system-from the child/ family to the infrastructure-financial gaps impact the effectiveness of child care teachers in meeting the developmental needs of the children in their care. These gaps fall under three primary categories:

a) Affordability,

b) Workforce Development and Retention, and

c) Community and Financial Support for the Healthy Growth of Infants through Early Adolescents.

Learning from these innovative building blocks, the CCCC continues to develop its 10-year plan with specific financial strategies for families of all incomes for child care, early education, and out-of-school-time. These strategies will:

1) maximize the impact of current public and private funding sources and

2) identify new sources of public and private funds to partner with parent fees and public subsidies.

In several ways, the infrastructure of governmental and not-for-profit organizations supports the ability of child care teachers to meet the needs of children and youth. However, several financial gaps impede this work at the community level.

Promoting and financially supporting best practice: While the elements of best practice are well documented, national research demonstrates that programs provide predominantly mediocre care to children and youth. Financial resources are the greatest impediment to our system providing consistently high quality care. However, other barriers include a disjointed higher educational system with few bridges from:

a) community based training to

b) community and technical colleges to

c) four-year colleges and universities.

In addition, the low wages for child care and out-of-school time child care teachers are a disincentive for them to pursue Associate's, Bachelor's, and Master's degrees. Many programs currently meet only the minimum needs of licensing support, technical assistance, referrals, training and education, assistance with budgeting and financial planning, and guidance in creating benefits and salary scales for child care teachers. The CCCC is working actively with the Governor on the NGA Moving Public Will grant, the most initiative, the Northwest Finance Circle, the Foundation for Early Learning, the Talaris Research Institute and other organizations that are working to increase the public's understanding of the social and economic benefits of child care, early learning, and out-of school-time care.

Readiness Assessment

State systems for assessing children as they enter kindergarten are expanding rapidly. It seems as though each week sees more and more states entering the assessment arena, intent on determining whether their children are "ready to learn" when they come to kindergarten. The goal one technical planning group broke new ground by defining not only what the important dimensions of "readiness" are but also what conditions are critical for supporting those dimensions. The five dimensions of early development and learning (physical and motor, social and emotional, approaches toward learning, language, and cognition and general knowledge) have become widely accepted, in one form or another. The three supporting conditions (having access to quality preschool programs, parents as children's first teachers, and appropriate nutrition and health care) have even been expanded upon by others in recent years.

With the change in administrations almost a year ago, we have seen an increasing emphasis at the federal level on reading as the central challenge of elementary schools, and preparing children to learn to read as the major goal of kindergartens and programs that precede kindergarten-especially the year or two immediately preceding kindergarten, which we usually call "preschool." These emphases, but suggest here that the early childhood field has yet to fully realize their implications for prekindergarten education, the myriad programs that preschool-age children experience in this country, and the assessment of school readiness.

The early childhood field has made tremendous strides in the science of measuring important aspects of children's early development and learning. A number of national studies-including FACES, ECLS-K, and, for younger children, the Early Head Start programme evaluation—have measured developmental constructs and supporting conditions not heretofore included in large-scale assessments.

In fact, whereas two decades ago, many people in this field despaired of ever having a sufficient number of good-quality instruments, the concern now is a glut of instruments, along with the challenging task of selecting among them. SERVE, for example, has recently published a compendium of assessment instruments. The compendium summarizes 39 commercially available instruments and, in an easy-to-use format, guides potential users to key features of each instrument that should be considered in selecting the instruments to use. Child Trends, working with Lisbeth Schorr and the Pathways Mapping Project, has compiled a compendium of measures used in national, state, and local data collections. It includes largely unpublished sources, while taking a different approach by providing item-level information. This compendium has the advantage of summarizing measures that have been used in data collections that may parallel data collections that states may want to launch for readiness assessment. As with the SERVE compilation, it evaluates the measures along a number of important criteria. No longer can we complain that measures either do not exist or are impossible to access. The challenge instead is one of sorting and sifting, to choose what will be most appropriate and useful for each state's or community's purpose.

Reading Practises

Schools have always focused on reading instruction in the early elementary years. Today, that focus appears even greater, and concerns about "pre-reading" extend the discussion to preschool and earlier. The current emphases for elementary school curricula have important implications for readiness assessment. At the July 2001 White House Summit on Early Childhood Cognitive Development, Secretary Paige noted the possible chain of events set off by failure to learn to read: children who can't do homework, have difficulty keeping up in other classes, are repeating grades, get misidentified as learning-disabled and shunted to special education classes, and drop out. There are three elements are crucial to the way about readiness:

— comprehensiveness
— embeddedness
— continuity.

The direct implication for states is that their assessment strategies should tap all five dimensions of children's development and learning. This may not be as hard as it sounds. The Early Childhood Longitudinal Study-Kindergarten Cohort (ECLS-K), as well as the birth cohort study (ECLS-B), includes measures that span the five dimensions. Interestingly, the Early Head Start national evaluation, although focusing on children younger than the preschool years, also includes measures that span the five dimensions of early development and learning and the conditions that support them.

Covering all the dimensions is a challenge, and none of the studies cited captures all dimensions equally well. Two main reasons are often given for this: Comprehensive assessment 1) requires extensive assessment, with potential risk of overly intruding on the time of children, parents, and teachers; and 2) means assessing areas for which the field often lacks reliable and valid measures. The areas of social-emotional development and approaches toward learning are typically the least-well measured. Nevertheless, it is a challenge that is important to meet head on, since a partial assessment runs the risk of creating a biased-or, at best, incomplete-view of states' and communities' progress toward their readiness goals. Assessment must also be designed to obtain data on the conditions supporting children's development described in the objectives accompanying the first goal. The FACES measures include a parent interview that taps a portion of the community conditions supporting readiness; but these need to be expanded. In fact, there is good reason to believe that the conditions supporting readiness to succeed in school extend well beyond the three areas outlined by the planning group. These conditions might include such elements as:

1) Child and family conditions (both protective and risk factors, which include child health conditions, family income, and family life conditions);
2) Community service provisions and their accessibility (including health, parenting education, child care and early education services, and the "readiness" of the schools); and
3) Systems capacity (such as the efficacy and efficiency with which the community infrastructure functions.)

Thus, readiness assessments as embedded in these supporting conditions. The strength of a community-based approach to defining and assessing children's level of preparation for success in school is that the community can ascertain-and influence—the measures of success employed by the schools. When considering statewide assessments, come to an interesting issue of what defines the "community. Child and family conditions impinge directly on each child's development. As with the dimensions of children's development and learning, the supporting conditions may also be tailored to what's important in each "community." They may include:

1) fewer families living in unsafe housing or violence-prone neighborhoods,
2) reduced incidence of child abuse and neglect,
3) increased parental confidence that their children have a bright future,
4) increased involvement of fathers in the lives of their children, and
5) healthy marriages.

This might be considered to be another element of the supporting conditions. It seems worth highlighting, however, since it refers to relationships among a potentially large number of supporting conditions that can extend over a number of years. The first five years of life can lend stability to the child's development through continuity of experiences with family and programs or the period can be disruptive to healthy development. Children who experience child care and other out-of-home care and education settings are at some risk of bouncing from one type of program to another. Programs can provide continuity through their service emphases, or they can be so different as to cause disruption as children move from one setting to another.

Developing a Broader Perspective

In a number of respects, readiness assessment—or, assessment of children's early development and learning upon entry into school—can be thought of as programme evaluation, but evaluation in a very special sense. Although kindergarten entry is the beginning of a long educational journey for each child, it also represents the culmination of his or her first five years of life. What children know, what they can do, what attitudes and inclinations they have—all are a function of the families they have lived in, the neighborhoods in which they have played, the many (or few) caring adults who have nurtured them (or not), and the programmes and activities they have participated in (or not).

America's children have taken ballet lessons, put up with bullies, enjoyed Sesame Street and Mister Rogers' Neighborhood, and been subject to violence and danger.

They have attended church, mosque, temple, or synagogue, or not. All of these, and the thousands of other experiences in children's early lives, contribute to their language, their cognitive and physical abilities, their emotions and social skills, and the way they approach new learning opportunities. The challenge is to find a practical assessment process that will capture the "outcomes" of these vast and varied experiences.

In "theory of change" about the first five years of life and what outcomes they should lead to, the expected outcomes look very much like the dimensions of early development and learning that now stand for readiness. It is for these reasons that put so much stress on finding the measures that do justice to the full and comprehensive dimensions of readiness and to administering them in a way that allows the results of this five-year process to be seen.

Teaching Children with Learning Difficulties

Individual cards with cue picture on reverse. The acquisition of sight vocabulary and letter sounds/names requires considerable rehearsal, and it is important to establish instant recognition. Fluency training, where the child works against the clock, requires about 2 minutes individual work daily and is very effective.

The child's own reading book should be taped. The child listens and follows text with finger. The tape should be stopped after each page. The child tries to re-read it alone. The child should play back the tape to identify unknown words. The child continues to use the tape for support until they can read the book unaided.

If reading is mechanical, oral or written comprehension work should be linked to the reading book to encourage reading for meaning e.g. comprehension questions, cloze procedure.

This can be an effective way of supporting the dyslexic reader providing they remain active in the process. Visual tracking is often a difficulty. Rather than a card marker, a line drawn on acetate is preferable because it doesn't block off the text below and the eye can scan more quickly to the word starting the next line.

Phonological Awareness

If the child's spelling has quite a few bizarre errors, check phonological awareness. Phonological training should precede phonic teaching. Hearing letter sounds in words Work on identification of :

1. Initial sounds
2. Final consonants
3. Medial vowels in consonant-vowel-consonant words.

The first two can be practised playing I Spy. (I spy something beginning / ending with...) The third can be practised using vowel cards or plastic letters, with the child selecting the letter they hear. Increase the difficulty by increasing the number of choices. Be aware that *i* and *e* are particularly prone to confusion.

Rhyme: This is an area of particular difficulty for many dyslexics. This can be taught through games e.g. matching rhyming pictures, pelmenism with rhyming pictures, and oral games such as I Spy (something that sounds like...) or Rhyming Riddles.

Many dyslexics find it very difficult to identify the

individual sounds in blends and to blend two or more sounds together. Phonic segmentation is breaking a word down into its constituant blends. Many of the activities can be used as 'fillers' at registration time or when changing for PE. There are many useful activities to develop phonological awareness in Sounds Linkage and Launch into Reading Success.

Along a similar line, Spelling Ladders is a written activity e.g. change 'hat' into 'men' in three steps (hat...mat...man...men). One of the Easylearn Phonics series of books is full of photocopiable examples of this activity. There are various structured programmes that develop phonological awareness as they teach reading and spelling. Phonological Awareness Training (PAT), Toe by Toe, Beat Dyslexia, Teaching Reading Through Spelling (TRTS). The last one is a very intensive individual programme which requires specific training. However there are structured worksheets that have been developed to accompany it (STRANDS) which could be used without doing the formal programme.

Spelling: This is the area of greatest difficulty for dyslexics. Errors tend to fall into two categories—phonic spelling and bizarre spelling. If the spelling is very phonic, it suggests that the pupil is stronger in the auditory mode than the visual mode. If the spelling is bizarre (some correct letters but inappropriately placed), it suggests the pupil is stronger in the visual mode than the auditory mode, (can remember something of how the word looks but lacks the auditory sequencing skills to 'hear' the correct order.) Learning spellings tends to require considerable rehearsal. Dyslexic children will generally require to be given fewer spellings to learn at a time and will need to revisit spellings previously learned. It is important to focus on high frequency words and to use a multi-sensory approach such as simultaneous oral spelling (SOS)—say the letter name as it is written (cursive script) and say the whole word. Repeat several times before moving on to a new word.

Those who are stronger in the visual than the auditory mode may do well using neuro-linguistic programming (NLP) where the child looks up and creates a visual image of the word (in chunks if it is a multi-syllabic word). These children will also be helped by recognising 'words within words' e.g. what (what hat?) brother (brothers are rot!) catch (catch the cat!).

Spelling patterns are more easily recognised by children whose visual mode is their relative strength. They are helped by linking the new word to a known letter pattern.

For those who are stronger in the auditory mode than the visual mode, remediation needs to be based on auditory strategies such as:

1. Changing the pronunciation of the word e.g. be-ca-use, fri-end, bus-i-ness
2. Spelling the word using a rhythm e.g. q-u-eue
3. Looking at the structure of words—roots, suffixes, prefixes, e.g. sign, signal, signature
4. Using mnemonics

Children should be taught to use hand prompts. By touching the tip of the left forefinger with the tip of the left thumb and extending the other three fingers out straight, the shape of a 'b' is formed. By doing the same with the right hand a 'd' is formed. By reciting the first few letters of the alphabet (a b c d) the child is reminded that b comes before d. We read from left to right so the left hand makes b and the right hand makes d. For letter formation, the child can be taught that if the 'round' comes before the 'stick' they start with the 'round'. If the 'stick' comes before the 'round' they start with the stick..

It is good practice to train children to try the word themselves before asking a teacher to write it for them. The teacher can then offer praise and encouragement for parts of the word correctly identified, e.g. if 'sed' was written for 'said', a small tick could be drawn above the 's' and the 'd' and the child praised for getting the first and last letters correct. The teacher can then write the full word for the child. In this way the supplying of spellings is turned into a teaching opportunity.

Writing: The use of cursive script reduces the incidence of letter reversals. Use of a lead—in stoke on the first letter of a word means that all letters begin in the same place i.e. on the line. Having to think of spelling, letter formation, punctuation and content all at the same time places enormous demands on a child with dyslexia and can lead to considerable frustration. Consideration should be given to alternative methods of recording when appropriate.

At the early stages of literacy development dictionaries are very slow to use. Consider use of a key word card where high frequency words are grouped alphabetically. Children can have this beside them whenever they write and it should help to reduce rehearsal of errors! Many children with dyslexia seem to 'freeze' when it comes to writing. They limit what they write to what they think they can spell. Specify times when 'spelling doesn't matter' and the aim is to get down as many ideas as possible.

It is too much to proof-read for everything in one go. Proof-read with a purpose, e.g. full stops and capital letters; word ommissions; key spellings. It is often difficult for children with dyslexia to track visually and they lose their place easily when copying from a board. They can be helped by:

1. writing lines in alternate colours
2. numbering each line
3. copying from worksheets rather than the board.

Reasons of School Drop-outs

School wastage has important long-term effects on patterns of adult illiteracy. It is widely recognized that children who drop out of school before acquiring basic literacy and numeracy skills frequently relapse into illiteracy. Estimates based on a simulation model project that 57 per cent of the illiterate adults (aged 15 and over) constituting the target population for literacy instruction in the less developed regions over the period 1995-2005 would comprise the backlog of adults who were illiterate at the beginning of the period.

Another 21 per cent would be children reaching age 15 during the period and who had no access to schooling, while 22 per cent more would be children reaching age 15 and dropping out of school before reaching Grade 5. One of the presumed benefits of repetition is to ensure that pupils in each grade have attained more or less the same level of learning and can learn at about the same pace. This assumption is frequently undermined, however, when teachers end up dealing with pupils of varying ages. Many teachers and school administrators consider it normal for substantial proportions of pupils to be held back. They take pride in high repetition rates and see them as evidence of their commitment to high standards. Other educators, however, see them as an indictment of the teaching that the retained pupils received. In any case, what some see as a yardstick of academic quality can have pedagogical, social and personal consequences that are quite destructive. Anecdotal evidence suggests that decisions to hold pupils back are sometimes made on capricious and arbitrary grounds that have little to do with actual pupil performance. Teachers often favour pupils who readily follow rules and give more attention to the brightest pupils at the expense of the others, including pupils who are competent but not outstanding.

A study carried out in rural primary schools in Honduras, found that 20 per cent of pupils with sufficient qualifications had not been promoted, while another study in rural Brazil found no significant relation between actual performance and promotion. School systems in many countries lack clear definitions and established procedures for assessing pupil performance and making promotion decisions. By operating in an elitist fashion and failing to be sensitive to the needs of many ordinary and low-achieving pupils, schools cease to be truly open and accessible to all. They become the property of a minority of highly motivated local elites and thus become alienated from the community as a whole. Schools that limit the prospects for success undermine the motivation of parents to send their children to school.

Maintaining policies that lead to repetition of grades by large numbers of pupils is expensive. The cost of repetition alone was estimated to total at least US$6 billion for all regions together, with Latin America and the Caribbean region accounting for about half of the total. The cost of total wastage in the first four grades was estimated to absorb some 16 per cent of public current expenditure on education in the less developed regions. These estimates should be viewed as minimal because they do not take into account capital expenditure on education, nor private spending. Regardless of its pedagogical effects, repeating grades is inefficient because it increases the per pupil cost of schooling without increasing the number of graduates produced. Resources devoted to a repeater are resources that could have been used either to permit another child to enter school or to improve the quality of instruction for pupils already there.

One of the premises of investment in education is that it makes an important and measurable contribution to the economic growth of society, in particular by improving the productivity of labour. A close parallel exists between the rate of economic growth of a country and the overall level of education of its active population. This correlation has been documented both in advanced industrial societies and in developing countries where the agricultural sector remains dominant. Whereas reliance on agriculture has frequently been a force for keeping children out of school, modern agricultural practices require more skilled, albeit fewer, workers. In view of the importance of the agricultural sector for the economy of most poor countries, it is clear that the persistence of substantial school wastage is contrary to the economic interest of these countries, especially since wastage tends to be more pronounced in rural than in urban areas.

Although the level of education is not the only factor involved in agricultural production, the failure to enable many rural young people to master basic skills undermines other initiatives to stimulate rural development. Children who drop out of school before acquiring sustainable reading and writing skills frequently relapse into illiteracy. Thus dropping out undermines efforts to reduce adult illiteracy—like trying to drain a sink that is being filled at the same time by the tap. Children and adolescents out of school in urban areas are also more vulnerable to the attractions of street life and organized gangs of children, which contributes to problems of delinquency and crime. Furthermore, school wastage promotes a 'culture of failure'. Repeaters thus become likely candidates for dropping out entirely. Children's success in school is generally believed to be primarily a function of their innate intellectual aptitudes. Yet, in the case of pupils who come from deprived home environments, their living conditions may considerably reduce their motivation and opportunities to learn, whatever their intellectual ability may be. Also, the language of instruction may put certain children at a distinct disadvantage. By disregarding these conditions and attributing poor academic performance to the assumed 'inability' of the child, the school merely reinforces discriminatory social conditions.

Data from UNESCO and other sources show that drop-out rates are highly sensitive to the national economic context. Studies in certain less developed countries, have shown a significant and positive correlation between drop-out rates and the percentage of people living below the poverty line, i.e. on less than $1 a day. For instance, as access to health services increases. As one would expect, children do better in school when they are healthy. Countries with similar social indices sometimes report quite different patterns of repetition, while countries at quite different levels of development tend to have dissimilar levels of dropout. It appears that drop-out rates are closely linked to the general state of a society—its level of economic and cultural development, how social services are distributed and attitudes toward education—while the repetition rates are largely determined by school policies.

Even when public schools are ostensibly free, parents must bear various direct costs to educate their children. Often, they must purchase school supplies and textbooks. While school uniforms may be a source of pride for pupils and their families, they can represent a major cost for parents with limited means. Developing countries frequently impose de facto tuition charges in the form of fees for registration, examinations and other services. In many cases these 'user fees' total many times the amount the government's expenditure per pupil. Public policy-makers can reduce these direct costs that families must bear to enrol their children in school through means such as subsidizing textbooks and transportation, providing essential school supplies and waiving school fees for pupils from very poor families. Recently, in response to the economic crisis, Indonesia obtained a rescue programme from the World Bank and the Asian Development Bank to help keep some 25 million Indonesian pupils in school over the next five years. Families also face indirect costs, primarily in the form of labour that the child would otherwise be performing if not enrolled in school. Thus, pupils in school cannot be taking care of younger siblings in the home or selling goods in the market or looking after farm animals or working in the fields. A study of school wastage conducted in twenty-four schools in the eleven counties of the State of Bahia in Brazil showed that the primary cause of school-drop-out was the need for the child to work to help support the family.

Both the direct and indirect costs of schooling are particularly important in the case of girls. When poor families conclude that they can afford to educate only some of their children, they tend to favour sons over daughters in the belief that it is more important for boys to be equipped to enter the job market. In some countries, it is common for the eldest daughter to drop out of school as soon as there are younger brothers and sisters for her to look after and she is unlikely to return to school even if the younger siblings, both male and female, enter school.

Lack of proximity to schools is an important cause of wastage, especially for younger children in rural areas who need a school close to their homes. Some countries are overcoming this obstacle by setting up community schools or 'branch' or 'feeder' schools connected to established schools. Even though these small schools often can offer only the first few primary grades, they can have a positive impact on access, especially for girls. A UNESCO survey in 1991 showed that the proportion of incomplete schools in rural areas was over 30 per cent in nearly half of the countries of sub-Saharan Africa and in one-third of the Arab States and countries in the Latin America and Caribbean region. However, the pupils who enter these incomplete schools often find it difficult to continue their schooling at a more distant location. If there is no provision of school transport or midday meals, only the most motivated families will continue sending their children to school away from the local community.

A few countries, such as Bhutan, Malaysia and Thailand, are overcoming this difficulty by providing limited boarding facilities for pupils who live great distances from school, but this solution is more often used for postprimary levels of education. Another approach to expanding access, used in the Philippines and Thailand, for example, is to employ 'mobile teachers' who travel by horseback or other means to reach pupils in remote areas. Yet another approach that is used in thinly populated areas is to permit teachers to teach several grades simultaneously—multigrade instruction. To be effective, this approach requires ample availability of teaching materials, since pupils must spend a good part of the school day working on their own or in small groups while the teacher is working with pupils in other 'grades'. The provision of adequate classrooms and teachers in accessible schools is an important condition for universal primary education, but other, complementary measures have proved necessary to ensure that all children actually attend school. Parents need to be encouraged and convinced to send their children to school and compulsory education laws need to be enforced.

Common sense suggests—and numerous studies have confirmed—that children are far more likely to be motivated to learn and to persist in school if the curricula and teaching methods are of high quality. By contrast, pupils who are bored and fail to see the connection between their personal lives and what they are taught in school become candidates for academic failure and, eventually, dropping out. There is much that can and must be done to improve the quality of instruction through a concerted strategy to improve the curricula, the training of teachers and the reorganization of the school to promote learning. There, school directors and programme supervisors devise an annual improvement plan to examine their needs, raise their standards and, in co-operation with teachers, evaluate their work.

Numerous studies have established that skilled

teaching has a strong positive impact on pupil achievement. A recent study in rural Pakistan found that investments that improve teacher quality and increase student exposure to teachers are likely to have higher returns in schooling effectiveness than those that improve physical infrastructure and equipment. Another recent large-scale research project in the United States found that the wide disparities in achievement between black and white pupils attending different schools were almost entirely accounted for by the qualifications of teachers. But improving the quality of teacher training requires more than imparting new pedagogical techniques. Instead, they believe that learning abilities are innate, so they tend to ascribe failure primarily to a pupil's low intelligence, lack of work or family background. These teachers regard their task as merely transmitting knowledge, rather than guiding pupils through a learning process. Such attitudes among teachers are often intensified by poor working conditions and the lack of any professional framework through which they could exchange experiences and learn from their peers. Also, teacher morale and salaries are low in many countries, which does not encourage them to seek to improve their skills.

Any systematic effort to reduce school wastage should include measures to enhance the skills and working conditions of classroom teachers, especially those who teach in the early grades where repetition is greatest. Both preservice and in-service teacher training should aim to equip teachers with a variety of practical strategies for helping pupils learn in a timely fashion. Teachers need to master pupil-centred approaches that recognize that each pupil has specific learning needs and requires a particular set of interventions. Various strategies can be employed to upgrade teachers' skills and attitudes and their capacities to introduce new curricular materials and teaching methods.

A number of countries, have found that school attendance can be improved and wastage reduced by organizing school calendars so that pupils in rural areas are not expected to attend school during planting and harvest seasons when their families need their labour. Similarly, the hours of the school day can be set to take account of the fact that some pupils, especially girls, must perform household chores. Classes that include pupils of different ages have been found, under certain conditions, to be an effective way of dealing with the fact that pupils develop at different paces, especially during the primary school years. When teachers have been trained to manage such classes and to take advantage of the instructional possibilities inherent in such diversity, they often find that retention becomes unnecessary.

A considerable body of literature demonstrates the advantages of "front loading" educational services to make sure that pupils get off to a good start in their schooling and build a strong base for future learning. A study in Madagascar, for instance, found strong correlations between pre-school education and lowered school wastage rates. In most developing countries, however, early childhood education is still considered to be a luxury and most such programmes are located in urban areas only. They are often considered by the personnel and the parents as a downward extension of schooling. Consequently, the personnel are not always sensitive to the developmental needs of pre-school children and force them prematurely into routine reading and writing.

Well-designed early childhood development programmes have proved to be effective in helping pupils from poor families to acquire some of the cultural attitudes and school-readiness skills that children from more affluent families learn in their homes. It is important, however, that such programmes be carried out by competent personnel with special training. Instructional methods should aim to awaken children's interest in learning rather than to push them to early acquisition of formal academic skills. The selection, competence and behaviour of teachers responsible for the entry grade should be a priority in efforts to combat wastage. School administrators would do well to assign the best teachers to work with the beginning pupils.

A number of countries have found ways to put more resources, including teaching time, into the early grades. One approach is to provide remedial measures for chronic repeaters. Intensive study in small groups and a belief in the pupils' innate possibilities are the hallmarks of this strategy, which targets the counties and schools with the biggest age-range per grade.

An estimated 10 per cent of all pupils have significant difficulties in learning at school. Children's disabilities and other learning difficulties may result from a number of factors: those within the child but also environmental factors such as poverty or lack of stimulation and school-related factors such as lack of good instructional materials, and inappropriate teaching and assessment standards. The very concept of 'special needs' has thus widened to include all children who are failing to benefit from school for whatever reasons. Special education is no longer a marginal issue and is now more commonly referred to as inclusive education or the 'one school for all' approach.

Efforts to Support Child Education

'No Child Left Behind' is a landmark in education reform designed to improve student achievement and change the culture of America's schools. Describes this law as the "cornerstone of my administration." Clearly, children are future, and, has expressed, "Too many of neediest children are being left behind." With passage of 'No Child Left Behind', Congress reauthorized the Elementary and Secondary Education Act (ESEA)—the principal federal law affecting education from kindergarten through high school. In amending ESEA, the new law represents a sweeping overhaul of federal efforts to support elementary and secondary education in the United States. It is built on four common-sense pillars:

- — accountability for results;
- — an emphasis on doing what works based on scientific research;
- — expanded parental options; and
- — expanded local control and flexibility.

Children who enter school with language skills and pre-reading skills are more likely to learn to read well in the early grades and succeed in later years. In fact, research shows that most reading problems faced by adolescents and adults are the result of problems that could have been prevented through good instruction in their early childhood years. It is never too early to start building language skills by talking with and reading to children. 'No Child Left Behind' targets resources for early childhood education so that all youngsters get the right start.

Under 'No Child Left Behind', each state must measure every public school student's progress in reading and math in each of grades 3 through 8 and at least once during grades 10 through 12. By school year 2007-2008, assessments in science will be underway. These assessments must be aligned with state academic content and achievement standards. They will provide parents with objective data on where their child stands academically.

'No Child Left Behind' requires states and school districts to give parents easyto-read, detailed report cards on schools and districts, telling them which ones are succeeding and why. Included in the report cards are student achievement data broken out by race, ethnicity, gender, English language proficiency, migrant status, disability status and low-income status; as well as important information about the professional qualifications of teachers. With these provisions, 'No Child Left Behind' ensures that parents have important, timely information about the schools their children attend-whether they are performing well or not for all children, regardless of their background.

In this new era of education, children will no longer be trapped in the dead end of low-performing schools. Under 'No Child Left Behind', such schools must use their federal funds to make needed improvements. In the event of a school's continued poor performance, parents have options to ensure that their children receive the high-quality education to which they are entitled. That might mean that children can transfer to higher-performing schools in the area or receive supplemental educational services in the community, such as tutoring, after-school programs or remedial classes.

Annual tests to measure children's progress provide teachers with independent information about each child's strengths and weaknesses. With this knowledge, teachers can craft lessons to make sure each student meets or exceeds the standards. In addition, principals can use the data to assess exactly how much progress each teacher's students have made and to better inform decisions about how to run their schools.

'No Child Left Behind' defines the qualifications needed by teachers and paraprofessionals who work on any facet of classroom instruction. It requires that states develop plans to achieve the goal that all teachers of core academic subjects be highly qualified by the end of the 2005-06 school year. States must include in their plans annual, measurable objectives that each local school district and school must meet in moving toward the goal; they must report on their progress in the annual report cards.

Today, more than $7,000 on average is spent per pupil by local, state and federal taxpayers. States and local school districts are now receiving more federal funding than ever before for all programs under 'No Child Left Behind': $23.7 billion, most of which will be used during the 2003-04 school year.

In exchange for the strong accountability, 'No Child Left Behind' gives states and local education agencies more flexibility in the use of their federal education funding. As a result, principals and administrators spend less time filling out forms and dealing with federal red tape. They have more time to devote to students' needs. They have more freedom to implement innovations and allocate resources as policymakers at the state and local levels see fit, thereby giving local people a greater opportunity to affect decisions regarding their schools' programs.

'No Child Left Behind' puts a special emphasis on implementing educational programs and practices that have been clearly demonstrated to be effective through rigorous scientific research. Federal funding will be targeted to support such programs. The Reading First program makes federal funds available to help reading teachers in the early grades strengthen old skills and gain new ones in instructional techniques that scientifically based research has shown to be effective. Since the Elementary and Secondary Education Act first passed Congress in 1965, the federal government has spent more than $242 billion through 2003 to help educate disadvantaged children. Yet, the achievement gap in this country between rich and poor and white and minority students remains wide.

According to the most recent National Assessment of Educational Progress (NAEP) on reading in 2000, only 32 percent of fourth-graders can read at a proficient level and thereby demonstrate solid academic achievement; and while scores for the highest-performing students have improved over time, those of America's lowest-performing students have declined. The good news is that some schools in cities and towns across the nation are creating high achievement for children with a history of low performance. If some schools can do it, then all schools should be able to do it.

Parents will know their children's strengths and weaknesses and how well schools are performing; they will have other options and resources for helping their children if their schools are chronically in need of improvement. Teachers will have the training and resources they need for teaching effectively, using curricula that are grounded in scientifically based research; annual testing lets them know areas in which students need extra attention. Principals will have information they need to strengthen their schools' weaknesses and to put into practice methods and strategies backed by sound, scientific research. Superintendents will be able to see which of their schools and principals are doing the best job and which need help to improve. School boards will be able to measure how their districts are doing and to measure their districts in relation to others across the state; they will have more and better information on which to base decisions about priorities in their districts.

Chief state school officers will know how the schools in their states and in other states are doing; they will be better able to pinpoint where guidance and resources are needed. Governors will have a yearly report card on how their states' schools are doing; they will be able to highlight accomplishments of the best schools and target help to those schools that are in need of improvement. Community leaders and volunteer groups will have information they can use to rally their members in efforts to help children and schools that need the most help.

Reports on individual schools are part of the annual district report cards, also known as local report cards. Each school district must prepare and disseminate annual local report cards that include information on how students in the district and in each school performed on state assessments. The report cards must state student performance in terms of three levels: basic, proficient and advanced. Achievement data must be disaggregated, or broken out, by student subgroups according to: race, ethnicity, gender, English language proficiency, migrant status, disability status and low-income status. The report cards must also tell which schools have been identified as needing improvement, corrective action or restructuring.

How can parents see these local report cards, which include school by-school data? States must ensure that the local districts make these local report cards available to the parents of students promptly and by no later than the beginning of the school year. The law requires that the information be presented in an "understandable and uniform format, and to the extend practicable, in a language that the parents can understand." States and districts may also distribute this information to the media for publicizing; post it on the Internet; or provide it to other public agencies for dissemination. Further, local school districts must notify parents if their child's school has been identified as needing improvement, corrective action or restructuring. In this event, districts must let parents know the options available to them.

What information is provided on state report cards? Each state must produce and disseminate annual report cards that provide information on student achievement in the state-both overall and broken out according to the same subgroups as those appearing on the district report cards listed above. State report cards include:

— State assessment results by performance level (basic, proficient and advanced), including (1) two-year trend data for each subject and grade tested; and (2) a comparison between annual objectives and actual performance for each student group.

— Percentage of each group of students not tested.

— Graduation rates for secondary school students and any other student achievement indicators that the state chooses.

— Performance of school districts on adequate yearly progress measures, including the number and names of schools identified as needing improvement.

— Professional qualifications of teachers in the state, including the percentage of teachers in the classroom with only emergency or provisional credentials and the percentage of classes in the state that are not taught by highly qualified teachers, including a comparison between high- and low-income schools.

In defining adequate yearly progress, each state sets the minimum levels of improvement-measurable in terms of student performance-that school districts and schools must achieve within time frames specified in the law. In general, it works like this: Each state begins by setting a "starting point" that is based on the performance of its lowest-achieving demographic group or of the lowest-achieving schools in the state, whichever is higher. The state then sets the bar-or level of student achievement—that a school must attain after two years in order to continue to show adequate yearly progress. Subsequent thresholds must be raised at least once every three years, until, at the end of 12 years, all students in the state are achieving at the proficient level on state assessments in reading/language arts and math.

In addition, the law requires states to identify for improvement those local education agencies that fail to make adequate yearly progress for two consecutive years or longer and to institute corrective actions. How are teachers or schools that do well rewarded? 'No Child Left Behind' requires states to provide state academic achievement awards to schools that close achievement gaps between groups of students or that exceed academic achievement goals. In addition, states must designate as distinguished schools those that have made the greatest gains in closing the achievement gap or in exceeding achievement goals.

'No Child Left Behind' supports parent involvement because research overwhelmingly demonstrates the positive effect that parent involvement has on their children's academic achievement. In the event a school is identified as needing improvement, corrective action or restructuring, the law requires the local education agency to notify parents accordingly and to explain to them how they can become involved in school improvement efforts. In any event, the law requires the same agency to provide parents with local report cards, which include data on each individual school in the district, as described earlier. Thus, parents have up-to-date information about their child's school, which they can use in whatever manner they choose to be involved. Parents may help their child's school in a number of ways, including: Attending parent-teacher meetings or special meetings to address academic problems at the school; volunteering to serve as needed; encouraging other parents to become involved; and learning about the school's special challenges, community resources and the 'No Child Left Behind' Act. In addition, parents should take advantage of the increased flexibility given local decision-makers by 'No Child Left Behind' and talk with their school board members, principals and other state and local education leaders about which programs they think will help their students the most. In addition, the law has other specific requirements on parent involvement that include the following:

— Each state education agency must support the collection and dissemination of information on effective parent involvement practices to local education agencies and schools.

— Schools that have schoolwide programs must involve parents in developing plans for such programs-that is, programs designed to raise the achievement of low-achieving students in high-poverty Title I schools by improving instruction throughout the entire school.

— The law provides for involvement of parents of private schools students served by various federal education programs such as Title I.

Although testing may be stressful for some students, testing is a normal and expected way of assessing what students have learned. The purpose of state assessments required under 'No Child Left Behind' is to provide an independent insight into each child's progress, as well as each school's. This information is essential for parents, schools, districts and states in their efforts to ensure that no child-regardless of race, ethnic group, gender or family income—is trapped in a consistently low-performing school.

'No Child Left Behind' requires that, by the 2005-06 school year, each state must measure every child's progress in reading and math in each of grades 3 through 8 and at least once during grades 10 through 12. In the meantime, each state must meet the requirements of the previous law reauthorizing ESEA for assessments in reading and math at three grade spans (3-5; 6-9; and

10-12). By school year 2007-2008, states must also have in place science assessments to be administered at least once during grades 3-5; grades 6-9; and grades 10-12. Further, states must ensure that districts administer tests of English proficiency-to measure oral language, reading and writing skills in English-to all limited English proficient students, as of the 2002-03 school year.

Students may still undergo state assessments in other subject areas (i.e., history, geography and writing skills), if and when the state requires it. 'No Child Left Behind', however, requires assessments only in the areas of reading/ language arts, math and science. It requires that all children be assessed. In order to show adequate yearly progress, schools must test at least 95 percent of the various subgroups of children, including their students with disabilities and those with limited English proficiency. States must provide reasonable accommodations for students with disabilities or limited English proficiency. For the latter, accommodations may include native-language versions of the assessment; however, in the area of reading and language arts, students who have been in U.S. schools for three consecutive years will be assessed in English. For more information on accommodations in a particular state, contact the appropriate state education agency.

State assessments are expected to measure how well students meet the state's academic standards, which define what students should know and be able to do in different subject areas at different grade levels. Under the previous reauthorization of the Elementary and Secondary Education Act in 1994, states were required to develop or adopt standards in mathematics and in reading or language arts; 'No Child Left Behind' requires states to do the same with science standards by 2006. Curriculum based on state standards should be taught in the classroom. If teachers cover subject matter required by the standards and teach it well, then students will master the material on which they will be tested-and probably much more. In that case, students will need no special test preparation in order to do well.

The point of state assessments is to measure student learning. A key principle of quality management is the importance of measuring what is valued. Such measures enable an organisation to identify where and how to improve operations. In the same manner, if schools and school systems are to continuously improve, they must measure growth in student achievement. After all, the core of all activity in schools and school systems is teaching and learning.

Annual state assessments required under 'No Child Left Behind' produce data on student performance at individual schools; and this information is used to gauge whether each and every school is meeting the state's standard of "adequate yearly progress." Parents can check progress made in improving student performance at their child's school by checking the annual district report card. If their school is not making adequate yearly progress and has been identified as needing improvement, corrective action or restructuring, 'No Child Left Behind' requires that districts notify parents and offer options.

Annual testing provides teachers with a great deal of information. For example, overall poor results could indicate that the curriculum needs to be reviewed and aligned with the content upon which state standards are based; poor results could also mean that teachers need to modify their instructional methods. Another likely indicator of the same problems would be if teachers saw poor performance by their students in certain areas. Test results could also help teachers to clarify those areas in which they may need professional development. Finally, teachers gain a great deal of information about the performance of individual students that enables them to meet the particular needs of every child.

Annual tests show principals exactly how much progress each teacher's students have made. They can use this information to guide decisions about program selection, curriculum arrangement, professional development for teachers and school resources they might need. Tests also show principals the strengths and weaknesses of students—in terms of the whole school, various subgroups and as individuals—and enable them to make plans that bolster strengths and address weaknesses.

Since 1969, National Assessment of Educational Progress (NAEP) has been the only nationally representative and continuing assessment of what American students know and can do in major academic subjects. Over the years NAEP has measured students' achievement in many subjects, including reading, mathematics, science, writing, history, civics, geography and the arts. Since 1992, the current NAEP reading assessment has been given in four different years to a nationally representative sample of fourth-grade students. NAEP provides a wealth of data about the condition of education in the United States. Under 'No Child Left Behind', as a condition of receiving federal funding, states are required to participate in the NAEP math and reading assessments for fourth—and eighth-grade students every two years, beginning in 2002-03. Resulting data will significantly increase information that parents-and others—can use to compare the performance of children in one state with that of children in another state.

Results of the most recent National Assessment of Educational Progress on reading showed that only 32 percent of the nation's fourth-graders performed at or above the proficient achievement level, thus demonstrating solid academic performance. And, while scores for the highest-performing students have improved over time, those of America's lowest-performing students have declined. Research has consistently identified the critical skills that young students need to learn in order to become good readers. Teachers across different states and districts have demonstrated that scientifically based reading instruction can and does work with all children. They have taught children-even those among the most difficult to educate-to become proficient readers by the end of third grade. Thus, the key to helping all children learn is to help teachers in each and every classroom benefit from the relevant research. That can be accomplished by providing professional development for teachers on the use of scientifically based reading programs; by the use of instructional materials and programs that are also based on sound scientific research; and by ensuring accountability through ongoing assessments.

Reading opens the door to learning about math, history, science, literature, geography and much more. Thus, young, capable readers can succeed in these subjects, take advantage of other opportunities (such as reading for pleasure) and develop confidence in their own abilities. On the other hand, those students who cannot read well are much more likely to drop out of school and be limited to low-paying jobs throughout their lives.

Reading is undeniably critical to success in today's society. Improving the reading skills of children is a top priority for leaders at all levels of government and business, as well as for parents, teachers and countless citizens who volunteer at reading programs across the nation. At the national level, 'No Child Left Behind' reflects this concern with the new program called Reading First. It is an ambitious national initiative designed to help every young child in every state become a successful reader. It is based on the expectation that instructional decisions for all students will be guided by the best available research. In recent years, scientific research has provided tremendous insight into exactly how children learn to read and the essential components for effective reading instruction.

Information to make that judgment will come from the states. 'No Child Left Behind' requires each state to:

1) prepare an annual report showing the greatest gains in reading achievement;
2) reduce the number of children in grades 1-3 who are reading below grade level; and
3) increase the percentage of children overall who are reading at grade level or above.

In order to fulfill these requirements, states must measure progress in reading skills for children in grades 1-2; and, as prescribed by 'No Child Left Behind', states have to ensure that all children in grades 3-8 are tested annually in reading. Results of these assessments should soon provide clear evidence of Reading First's effectiveness. There is good cause for confidence, since the programs and practices that Reading First supports must already have been demonstrated as effective, based on solid scientific research.

For too many years, too many schools have experimented with lessons and materials that have proven to be ineffective—at the expense of their students. Under 'No Child Left Behind', federal support is targeted to those educational programs that have been demonstrated to be effective through rigorous scientific research. Reading First is such a program. Programs and practices grounded in scientifically based research are not fads or untested ideas; they have proven track records of success. By funding such programs, 'No Child Left Behind' encourages their use, as opposed to the use of untried programs that may later turn out to be fads. Furthermore, 'No Child Left Behind''s accountability requirements bring real consequences to those schools that continually fail to improve student achievement as a result of using programs and practices for which there is no evidence of success. Such schools would be identified as needing improvement and required to make changes as outlined in the section on Accountability, including using education programs that are grounded in scientifically based research. To say that an instructional program or practice is grounded in scientifically based research means there is reliable evidence that the program or practice works. To obtain reliable evidence about a reading strategy or instructional practice, an experimental study may be done that involves using an experimental/control group design to see if the method is effective in teaching children to read. 'No Child Left Behind' sets forth rigorous requirements to ensure that research is scientifically based. It moves the testing of educational practices toward the medical model used by scientists to assess the effectiveness of medications, therapies and the like. Studies that test random samples of the population and that involve a control group are scientifically controlled.

In 2002, the Department of Education's Institute of Education Sciences (IES) established the What Works Clearing house to provide a central, independent and trusted source of scientific evidence on what works in education for parents, educators, policymakers and anyone else who is interested. All of the research collected and conducted by the clearing house follows the same high scientific standards as those used for reading research and will be available via the Internet from the clearing house or through the Department's Web site. Parents may be able to use this information to find out about program and curricula selection at their child's school. The seven topics chosen for systematic review in the first year of the What Works Clearing house's operation reflect a wide range of our nation's most pressing education issues. They are:

— Interventions for Beginning Reading;

— Curriculum-based Interventions for Increasing K-12 Math Achievement;

— High School Dropout Prevention;

— Peer-Assisted Learning in Elementary Schools: Reading, Mathematics and Science Gains;

— Programs for Increasing Adult Literacy;

— Interventions to Reduce Delinquent, Disorderly and Violent Behavior, in and out of School; and

— Interventions for Elementary English Language Learners: Increasing English Language Acquisition and Academic Achievement.

Over time, as the clearinghouse begins to produce its

reports on these issues, parents will be able to ask their principal, teachers and school board members about the extent to which they select programs and curricula that the research has determined to be effective. Under 'No Child Left Behind', educators are expected to consider the results of relevant scientifically based research-whenever such information is available—before making instructional decisions.

'No Child Left Behind' requires local school districts to ensure that all teachers hired to teach core academic subjects in Title I programs after the first day of the 2002-03 school year are highly qualified. In general a "highly qualified teacher" is one with full certification, a bachelor's degree and demonstrated competence in subject knowledge and teaching. The act also calls for all teachers of the core academic subjects to be highly qualified by the end of school year 2005-06. 'No Child Left Behind' (ESEA, Title II) provides federal funding to states and districts for activities that will strengthen teacher quality in all schools, especially those with a high proportion of children in poverty.

The great majority of Title II funds, $2.9 billion in 2003-an increase of 39 percent since President Bush took office-is for the Improving Teacher Quality State Grants program. Funding can be used to support a wide array of activities, including interventions for teacher professional development, so long as the activities are grounded in scientifically based research. Because communities nationwide face such a variety of needs when it comes to teacher quality, the law gives schools and districts a great deal of flexibility in how the money is spent. It also holds them accountable for the proper and effective use of the funds. In addition to the state grants program, Title II includes funding for other teacher quality-related grant programs. This year the Transition to Teaching program will allocate nearly $42 million to states, school districts and nonprofit groups to help thousands of outstanding candidates enter teaching

Bibliography

Baxter, P. M., "Psychology: A guide to reference and information sources", Englewood, CO: Libraries Unlimited, 1993.

Damon, W. (Ed.), *Handbook of child psychology* (5th ed., Vols. 1-4). New York: Wiley, 1998.

Friedman, H. S. (Ed.), *Encyclopedia of mental health* (Vols. 1-3). San Diego, CA: Academic Press, 1998.

Groth-Marnat, G., *Handbook of psychological assessment* (3rd ed.). New York: Wiley, 1997.

International review of industrial and organizational psychology, New York: Wiley, 1994.

Kadzin, A. E. (Ed.), *Encyclopedia of psychology* (Vols. 1-8). New York: Oxford University Press, 2000.

Maddox, T. (Ed.) "Tests: A Comprehensive reference for assessments in Psychology, Education, and Business (4th ed.)", Austin, TX: Pro-Ed, 1997.

Palo Alto, "Annual Review of Psychology", *CA: Annual Reviews,* 1951, 1953.

Sheehy, N., Chapman, A. J., & Conroy, W. (Eds.), *Biographical dictionary of psychology,* London: Routledge, 1997.

Sternberg, R. J. (Ed.). Encyclopedia of human intelligence (Vols. 1-2). New York: Macmillan. (XBF 431 .E59 1994)

Index